Root Cause Analysis

Simplified Tools and Techniques

Also available from ASQ Quality Press:

Business Process Improvement Toolbox
Bjørn Andersen

Success Through Quality: Support Guide for the Journey to Continuous Improvement
Timothy J. Clark

Quality Problem Solving
Gerald F. Smith

Mapping Work Processes
Dianne Galloway

101 Good Ideas: How to Improve Just About Any Process
Karen Bemowski and Brad Stratton, editors

Root Cause Analysis: A Tool for Total Quality Management
Paul F. Wilson, Larry D. Dell, and Gaylord F. Anderson

Principles of Quality Costs: Principles, Implementation, and Use, Third Edition
ASQ Quality Costs Committee, Jack Campanella, editor

The Certified Quality Manager Handbook
ASQ Quality Management Division

To request a complimentary catalog of ASQ Quality Press publications, call 800-248-1946, or visit our web site at qualitypress.asq.org

Root Cause Analysis

Simplified Tools and Techniques

Bjørn Andersen
Tom Fagerhaug

ASQ Quality Press
Milwaukee, Wisconsin

Root Cause Analysis: Simplified Tools and Techniques
Bjørn Andersen and Tom Fagerhaug

Library of Congress Cataloging-in-Publication Data

Andersen, Bjørn.
    Root cause analysis : simplified tools and techniques / Bjørn
Andersen, Tom Fagerhaug.
        p.   cm.
    Includes bibliographical references and index.
    ISBN 0-87389-466-9 (alk. paper)
    1. Total quality management. 2. Problem solving. 3. Quality
control. I. Fagerhaug, Tom, 1968– . II. Title.
HD62.15.A53 2000
658.4'013--dc21   99-42486
                            CIP

10 9 8 7 6 5 4 3

ISBN 0-87389-466-9

Acquisitions Editor: Ken Zielske
Project Editor: Annemieke Koudstaal
Production Administrator: Shawn Dohogne

ASQ Mission: The American Society for Quality advances individual and organizational performance excellence worldwide by providing opportunities for learning, quality improvement, and
knowledge exchange.

Attention: Bookstores, Wholesalers, Schools and Corporations:
ASQ Quality Press books, videotapes, audiotapes, and software are available at quantity discounts
with bulk purchases for business, educational, or instructional use. For information, please contact ASQ Quality Press at 800-248-1946, or write to ASQ Quality Press, P.O. Box 3005,
Milwaukee, WI 53201-3005.

To place orders or to request a free copy of the ASQ Quality Press Publications Catalog, including
ASQ membership information, call 800-248-1946. Visit our web site at www.asq.org, or
qualitypress.asq.org

Printed in the United States of America

 Printed on acid-free paper

Quality Press
611 East Wisconsin Avenue
Milwaukee, Wisconsin 53202
Call toll free 800-248-1946
www.asq.org
http://qualitypress.asq.org
http://standardsgroup.asq.org
http://e-standards.asq.org
E-mail: authors@asq.org

Contents

4   Tools for Possible Cause Generation and Consensus Reaching   39

5   Tools for Possible Cause and Data Collection   61

6 Tools for Possible Cause Analysis   77

7 Tools for Cause-and-Effect Analysis   105

Preface

"How do you like your job?"

Ask this question of almost anyone, and most people will answer by focusing not on the positive aspects of their livelihood, but rather on opportunities for improvement. On the whole, people take for granted things that work, and want to improve those that don't. Such is the attitude (and rightfully so!) of those involved in quality improvement work.

The starting point of such improvement efforts is generally a problem experienced—and recognized—by one or more people, all with a common goal: to solve the problem. And a prerequisite to solving that problem is finding—and eliminating—its *root cause*. Only by doing so can you be sure that the problem is truly solved and that it won't blindside you again next week.

To get to the root of the problem efficiently and thereby improve a process, effective problem-solvers use something called *root cause analysis*.

Root causes can be uncovered and analyzed by using a number of approaches, techniques, and tools that help the problem-solver get to the heart of the problem and find its root cause(s). Some such tools are generic and can be used in many applications; others are suited solely for root cause analysis.

Several excellent books about root cause analysis are available, most of which tend to lump the concept of root cause analysis into the larger picture of total quality management (TQM). Few texts focus on these tools and explain how they combine to make up a powerful toolbox for root cause analysis. Furthermore, many such books assume that the reader is well versed in the jargon and content of TQM and continuous improvement. As such, the presentations of root cause analysis are far more complex than they need to be.

Root cause analysis is best suited for the average employee and is not reserved for the organization's quality manager. The results from using it are most effective when it is applied in groups of caring employees who want to improve their work situation and the products or services they generate. To make the art of root cause analysis more accessible to a larger audience, this book starts from scratch and gradually builds toward the objective of educating the reader in the basic skills of root cause analysis. Furthermore, this book does not address how to eliminate the root cause once it is found, or problem solving in general.

The book discusses many different tools for root cause analysis, and presents these tools using an easy-to-follow structure: a general description of the tool, its purpose and typical applications, the procedure when using it, an example of its use, a checklist to help you make sure it is applied properly, and different forms and templates that can be copied from the book. The examples are generic business examples that everyone should be able to recognize. Because this is not meant to be an academic book, you will not find the usual literature references scattered throughout. However, to probe more deeply into some subjects, books treating different aspects of root cause analysis in more detail have been listed at the end of the book. In this section, you'll also find a list of software that you can apply at different stages of the root cause analysis.

The layout of the book has been designed to help speed your learning. Throughout, we have split the pages into two halves. The top half presents key concepts using brief language—almost keywords—and the bottom half uses examples to help explain the concepts. A navigation aid in the margin of each page simplifies navigating the book and searching for specific topics when the book is used as a root cause analysis dictionary.

The book is suited for employees and managers at any organizational level in any type of industry, including service, manufacturing, and public sector.

Our thanks to all the people who have inspired the writing of this book, including colleagues, classroom participants in our training courses, and companies with which we have worked.

Bjørn Andersen
Tom Fagerhaug
Trondheim, October 1, 1999

Practical Problem Solving

This chapter sets the stage for the ensuing presentation of problem solving and root cause analysis. In it, we first define a problem, then give specific examples that illustrate the nature and types of problems that are discussed in this text. We discuss the different levels of causes for problems, and introduce a general approach to practical problem solving.

Definition of a Problem

"Problem, a question proposed for solution"
(*Webster's Revised Unabridged Dictionary*)

"A problem is a state of difficulty that needs to be resolved."
(*Wordnet*)

These definitions suggest two characteristics of a problem that are important in this context:

- Having a problem is by nature a state of affairs plagued with some difficulty or undesired status.

- A problem represents a challenge that encourages solving to establish more desirable circumstances.

TYPES OF PROBLEMS

From the definitions of *problem* given above, it is evident that a problem can occur in any sphere of a person's life and take any form and shape. There may be practical problems in your private life, personal problems in your work situation, organizational problems within your department, and so on. This book deals with the general topic of root cause analysis and problem solving and is, as such, not limited to attacks on certain *types* of problems. Rather, the approaches described here can apply to almost *any* kind of problem.

The examples and cases used throughout the book deal exclusively with problems that can occur within organizations. Our purpose in writing this book is a desire to help organizations solve problems that hinder their performance.

We are convinced that the tools can also apply to the parent who wants to spend more time with family or in solving personal problems. Therefore, if you wish to use the book to solve other types of problems, simply follow the instructions and adapt the lessons from the business-focused examples to your situation.

How to Solve a Problem

Beneath every problem lies a cause for that problem. Therefore, when trying to solve a problem, consider this approach:

1. Identify the cause (or causes) of the problem.

2. Find ways to eliminate these causes and prevent them from recurring.

Depending on the problem, this two-step approach can seem deceptively simple. Indeed, it is easy to underestimate the effort it sometimes takes to find the causes of a problem. Once you've established the true causes, however, eliminating them is a much easier task. Hence, identifying a problem's *cause* is paramount.

PROBLEM EXAMPLES

A sawmill periodically suffered severe problems of inaccuracy when cutting lumber to different dimensions. "Experts" launched varying theories as to the causes for this, but the problems persisted. After thoroughly assessing the situation, the parties assigned to pinpoint the reasons for the deviations found the cause to be highly varying air temperature and humidity, due to a poorly functioning air conditioning unit.

A car dealership had reorganized its operations to allow each employee to specialize in certain areas—that is, sales, after-sales service, financing, and so on. One of the salespersons occasionally lost a sale because the credit evaluation undertaken by the finance department took too long, and the customer took his business elsewhere. It turned out that the person responsible for the credit checks deliberately stalled the process because he felt overlooked when the specialized salespersons were selected.

Dimensional variation among lamp holders from certain suppliers caused a lot of rework for a lamp manufacturer. Adjustments that needed to be made to the lamp holders to ensure proper installation were estimated to cost more than $200,000 annually. Meanwhile, the procurement manager was pleased with himself because he managed to reduce purchasing costs by about $50,000 the previous year by soliciting offers from many suppliers and buying from the one who offered the lowest price!

Different Levels of Causes

A problem is often the result of *multiple* causes, at different "levels." This means that some causes affect other causes that, in turn, create the visible problem. Causes can be classified as one of the following:

- Symptoms: these are not regarded as actual causes, but rather as signs of existing problems.

- First level causes: causes that *directly* lead to a problem.

- Higher level causes: causes that lead to the first level causes. While they do not *directly* cause the problem, higher level causes form links in the chain of cause-and-effect relationships that ultimately create the problem.

Examples of the levels of causes follow.

EXAMPLES OF THE DIFFERENT LEVELS OF CAUSES

Consider a paper producer that is having problems complying with the environmental regulations that apply to his industry. The industry's regulatory body has become aware of this situation and is constantly monitoring—and occasionally fining—the company for any breaches.

This problem could be defined as "unacceptable discharges of pollutants to water and air." With regard to the different levels of causes presented above, this problem is a result of the following causes:

- The *symptoms* are the fines issued by the regulatory body. Because the paper producer does not have an operating system for measuring the discharges, these fines represent the only way in which the company can detect occurrences of the problem. The fines can therefore be used as a "symptometer" that can be monitored to determine whether the problem has been eliminated or still recurs (much like a thermometer is used to monitor the presence of a fever, which indicates an inflammation).

- The *first level cause* for the unacceptable discharges was that the company was slow to identify regulatory changes that affected its operations.

- More important, a chain of *higher level causes* ultimately cost the company large sums in fines. These higher level causes included the lack of an environmental management system, operating in a purely reactive mode, and the absence of an environmental impact strategy.

Find the Root Cause!

The highest level cause of a problem is called the **root cause**:

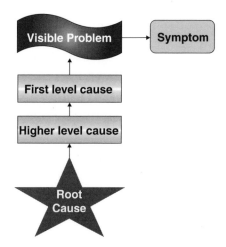

The root cause is "the evil at the bottom" that sets in motion the cause-and-effect chain that creates the problem(s).

TWO EXAMPLES OF ROOT CAUSES

In the example of the paper producer, the highest level cause, and thus the root cause for unacceptable discharges, was that the company had no environmental impact strategy. Such a strategy would probably have made the company more proactive regarding this issue: it might have paid more attention to new regulations and avoided illegal discharges.

When a hair dressing salon had to pay damages to customers because their hair was dyed the wrong color, the root cause was not that the hairdressers were poorly trained. Neither was the reason, as some employees claimed, that so little time was set aside for each customer that it led to sloppiness. The true root cause finally was discovered: the person who helped clean the salon returned opened bottles of dye to the wrong shelves. Why? Because she was color-blind and could not read the bottles.

You might find some of these root causes a little far-fetched. If so, take note of them even more. Problems such as these discussed here, which involve a number of different people and technical systems, are a cornucopia of different causes linked together in highly complex interrelationships. Consider the problems you face most often in your own organization—there could be equally unusual root causes at the heart of those problems! Again, the key issue is finding the root cause, be it extraordinary or commonplace.

Eliminate the Root Cause!!

The discussion so far leads to the key recommendation of eliminating the true root cause(s). Other approaches might provide some temporary relief, but will never produce a lasting solution.

- If you attack and remove only the symptoms, the situation can become worse. The problem will still be there, but there will no longer be an easily recognized symptom that can be monitored.

- Eliminating first or higher level causes can temporarily alleviate the problem, but the root cause will eventually find another way to manifest itself, in the form of another problem.

When you have removed the root cause, monitor the symptoms to help ensure that the problem will not recur.

ROOT CAUSE ANALYSIS AND PROBLEM SOLVING

So far, we have discussed the concept of a problem and the causes for problems. When we follow the chain of cause-and-effect behind a problem to its end, we discover the *root cause*. This can very well be the cause of many different problems, and it is most important to find and eliminate it.

The process of problem solving involves a number of steps, as illustrated on the following page. Important steps on the road to a solved problem are problem identification, problem definition, problem understanding, cause identification, cause elimination, and monitoring for recurrence. Each of these steps poses different challenges and every one can be tricky at times. However, we maintain that finding the root cause is the crux of solving a problem. Without the root cause, there can be no lasting solution.

While we will present one possible approach to practical problem solving, the emphasis of this book is on root cause analysis. For more comprehensive coverage of different problem solving approaches, see the additional resources listed at the end of the book.

A Problem Solving Process

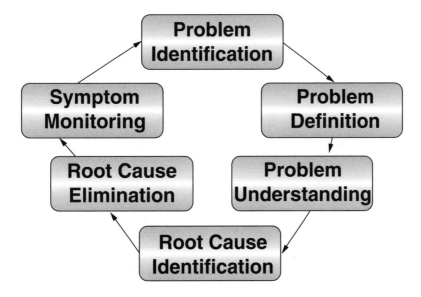

THERE ARE MANY DIFFERENT PROBLEM SOLVING APPROACHES

The process for problem solving shown above is just one of many such models. Some emphasize the importance of testing and evaluating solutions before making them permanent, others focus on involving those who know the problem best in solving it, while some point out the importance of seeing the problem solving as part of a larger improvement effort. Another well-known approach is the Deming Wheel, or the plan, do, check, and act cycle:

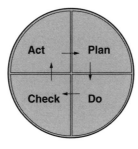

The Deming Wheel describes a systematic and continuous problem-solving approach. In the four phases, respectively, the problem is analyzed, rectifying measures are undertaken, the effects of these are evaluated, and the process is modified according to the activities that were confirmed to give results.

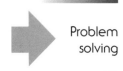

Problem
solving

Root cause
analysis

Problem
understanding

Possible cause
generation
and consensus
reaching

Problem and
cause
data collection

Possible cause
analysis

Cause-and-
effect
analysis

Tool selection

Case Business
Quality Travel

The Steps in Problem Solving

The content or purpose of each step in the problem-solving process is as follows:

- First, recognize that there is a problem. If you perceive the situation as normal, it will never improve.

- Then, call the problem by its real name; everyone affected by it must agree about this definition of it.

- Next, work to thoroughly understand the nature of the problem, as this forms the basis for ultimately solving it.

- As discussed, find the root cause.

- Only then are you able to attack—and ultimately eliminate— the root cause and thus prevent the problem from recurring.

- Lastly, monitor the symptoms signaling the presence of the problem to ensure success.

SOME PROBLEMS AREN'T WORTH THE TROUBLE IT TAKES TO SOLVE THEM

As you can see by the number of steps in a systematic approach to problem solving, the process can take some time and resources to accomplish the goal. Problems of minor importance, or of such a nature that they will likely go away by themselves given time, should not be the subject of such a comprehensive effort. It is simply not worth it, as the gains from removing the problem are less than the costs of completing the process to remove it.

Likewise, it is unproductive to apply a complicated problem-solving process to commonplace problems we already know how to solve.

However, when you perceive the problem as important and don't know its nature or causes, attack it systematically to ensure that you find the root cause and ultimately eliminate the problem for good. In such cases, the problem-solving process makes sense and the root cause analysis presented in the next chapters will be important.

Root Cause Analysis

So far, we have discussed problem solving in general, and the importance of root cause analysis in practical problem solving. In this chapter, we define the nature of root cause analysis, how it is performed, and the different detailed approaches, techniques, and tools used to analyze the concept. This chapter presents the *contents* of the toolbox of root cause analysis; chapters 3 through 7 describe these tools in more detail.

A Definition of Root Cause Analysis

As far as we can determine, there is no generally accepted definition of what root cause analysis is. Therefore, we offer the following as a *possible* definition, one that at least communicates what is meant by the concept:

"Root Cause Analysis is a structured investigation that aims to identify the true cause of a problem, and the actions necessary to eliminate it."

While this sounds fairly straightforward, you will soon see that root cause analysis is not conducted using a single tool or strategy, but rather a number of tools, often used in combination.

ROOT CAUSE ANALYSIS IN A LARGER CONTEXT

Taking a scholarly perspective, it is interesting to study which fields have led to the development of different concepts and ideas. The roots of root cause analysis, for example, can be traced to the broader field of Total Quality Management, or TQM. TQM has developed in different directions more or less simultaneously. One such direction is the development of a number of problem analysis, problem solving, and improvement tools. Today, TQM possesses a large toolbox of such techniques; root cause analysis is an integral part of this toolbox.

As indicated previously, root cause analysis is part of a more general problem-solving process. Further, problem solving is an integral part of continuous improvement. As such, root cause analysis is one of the core building blocks in an organization's continuous improvement efforts. There are many books dealing with continuous improvement, so we won't cover this topic here. However, we feel it is important to keep in mind that root cause analysis in itself will not produce any results. It must be made part of a larger problem-solving effort, part of a conscious attitude that embraces a relentless pursuit of improvements at every level and in every department or business process of the organization.

What Is Root Cause Analysis?

Root cause analysis is a collective term used to describe a wide range of approaches, tools, and techniques used to uncover causes to problems.

Some of the approaches are more geared toward identifying the true root causes than others; some are more general problem-solving techniques, while others simply offer support for the core activity of root cause analysis. Some tools are characterized by a structured approach, while others are more creative (and haphazard) in nature.

The point is not to learn and apply all these tools, but rather to become acquainted with the root cause analysis toolbox and apply the *appropriate* technique or tool to address a specific problem.

ROOT CAUSE ANALYSIS IS NOT THE ONLY OVERARCHING CONCEPT

If you are confused by the fact that root cause analysis is not a streamlined process of a fixed number of steps, there might be some consolation in that many of the toolbox techniques of TQM are overarching concepts. Some of the more important overarching concepts are

- Problem solving

- Business process reengineering or improvement

- Benchmarking

- Continuous improvement

All of these are often presented as if they were single tools, while in fact they cover a varying number of individual tools that are applied in a structured manner.

Problem solving

Root cause analysis

Problem understanding

Possible cause generation and consensus reaching

Problem and cause data collection

Possible cause analysis

Cause-and-effect analysis

Tool selection

Case Business Quality Travel

Groups of Root Cause Analysis Tools

We have grouped the different root cause analysis tools according to their purpose (and at which point they are typically used) for these reasons:

1. There are so many tools that it is necessary to maintain clarity throughout the presentation of them.

2. They naturally fall into categories of tools that serve slightly different purposes.

The groups of tools, according to their purpose, are

- Problem understanding
- Possible cause generation and consensus reaching

- Problem and cause data collection
- Possible cause analysis
- Cause-and-effect analysis

DIFFERENT MEANS TO THE SAME END

These five groups of tools contribute in their own way to the root cause analysis. Some are best applied sequentially, others can be applied at many different points in the analysis.

- Problem understanding: methods that help get to the bottom of a problem. This phase focuses on understanding the nature of the problem, and is a first step before starting the analysis.

- Possible cause generation and consensus reaching: generic tools that can be applied at different stages in the analysis. Brainstorming can help generate ideas about possible causes. Since the analysis normally is carried out in groups, methods that help you arrive at consensus solutions are also useful.

- Problem and cause data collection: these generic tools and techniques are used to systematically and efficiently collect data related to a problem and its probable cause.

- Possible cause analysis: tools used for making the most of the data collected about the problem. When analyzing the same data from different angles, different conclusions might emerge. Some conclusions may not uncover the problem's causes, so it is important to have several data analyzing tools available.

- Cause-and-effect analysis: the heart of root cause analysis. Root cause analysis is not one single approach, and neither is this group of tools. You can use these tools to more deeply analyze the problem's root cause(s).

The Individual Root Cause Analysis Tools

Problem Understanding

- Flowcharts: charts used to "paint a picture" of business processes

- Critical incident: an elegant approach used to explore the most critical issues in a situation

- Spider chart: a comparison chart used to benchmark problems

- Performance matrix: used to help determine the importance of problems or causes

Possible Cause Generation and Consensus Reaching

- Brainstorming: a formal approach that can be applied throughout the root cause analysis when multiple ideas are required

- Brainwriting: in effect, a written brainstorming session

- Nominal group technique: a technique used to help a group prioritize different alternatives—for example, problem causes

- Paired comparisons: a technique used to reach consensus by allowing participants to choose between two competing alternatives

Problem and Cause Data Collection

- Sampling: used to collect data on a large population by collecting only a small sample

- Surveys: used to collect data about opinions and attitudes from customers, employees, and so on

- Check sheet: a useful approach that systematically collects data based on predefined sheets that are applied throughout the collection period

Possible Cause Analysis

- Histogram: an easy-to-use visual diagram that helps identify patterns or anomalies

- Pareto chart: another visual tool used to illustrate which dominant causes generate the most effects

Problem solving

Root cause analysis

Problem understanding

Possible cause generation and consensus reaching

Problem and cause data collection

Possible cause analysis

Cause-and-effect analysis

Tool selection

Case Business Quality Travel

Problem
solving

Root cause
analysis

Problem
understanding

Possible cause
generation
and consensus
reaching

Problem and
cause
data collection

Possible cause
analysis

Cause-and-
effect
analysis

Tool selection

Case Business
Quality Travel

- Scatter chart: used to illustrate relationships between two causes or other variables in the problem situation

- Relations diagram: a tool used to identify logical relationships between different ideas or issues in a complex or confusing situation

- Affinity diagram: a chart approach that helps identify seemingly unrelated ideas, causes, or other concepts so they might collectively be explored further

Cause-and-Effect Analysis

- Cause-and-effect chart: an easily applied tool used to analyze possible causes to a problem

- Matrix diagram: a visual technique for arranging pieces of information according to certain aspects

- Five whys: an approach used to delve ever more deeply into causal relationships

Each of these tools and techniques is described in detail in chapters 3 through 7.

Conducting a Root Cause Analysis

Root cause analysis is a highly versatile analysis approach. These are some useful hints for carrying out this analysis:

- Many of the individual root cause analysis tools can be used by a single person. Nevertheless, the outcome is generally better when applied in a group of people who work together to find the problem causes.

- Those ultimately responsible for removing the identified root cause(s) should be prominent members of the analysis team that sets out to uncover them.

- Treat the titles of the groups of tools as indicative of their primary purpose. During the analysis, apply tools and approaches with which the team is familiar and that seem to fit.

WHICH TOOL TO USE WHEN

The sheer number of groups of tools, and certainly the individual tools that are available for a root cause analysis, can be enough to dissuade anyone from embarking on the analysis. Of course, this is not the purpose of presenting such a comprehensive collection of techniques. Rather, the objective is to demonstrate the vast opportunities that are open to you, even if one approach fails, by providing you with many different angles into the analysis.

In chapter 4, we outline guidelines for the selection of the right tool based on the situation you are facing and what you want to accomplish.

Let us again emphasize that we do not encourage you to memorize all these tools just to be sure you know them. Instead, become familiar with a few techniques that seem to produce results. If the initial collection fails or seems inadequate for the problem at hand, look more closely at other techniques that might supplement the ones you already know. Given time, you will learn to appreciate the various tools recognize their strengths and weaknesses, and develop your own customized approach to root cause analysis.

Tools for Problem Understanding

So far, we have laid the groundwork for the details of the root cause analysis. In this and the following chapters, we present each of the different tools and techniques briefly mentioned in chapter 2. We have adhered to a common structure for all tools: a general description of the tool, its purpose and typical applications, the procedure when using it, an example of its use, a checklist to help ensure it is applied properly, and forms and templates that can be photocopied from the book. This chapter deals specifically with how to gain a solid understanding of the problem that needs to be solved.

Problem Understanding

To ensure that your root cause analysis efforts are directed at the right problem, you must first *understand* the problem. The tools to help you do this are

- Flowchart

- Critical incident

- Spider chart

- Performance matrix

THE IMPORTANCE OF PROBLEM UNDERSTANDING

A newspaper printing company, fully owned by the newspaper it printed, also took on printing jobs for external customers. There were often scheduling problems when planning the printing of the newspaper (including second editions in cases of breaking news, advertising sections for the following day, and so on) and combining these with the external jobs. As a result, overtime was paid to complete all jobs. To attack this problem, the printing company invested in a sophisticated, computerized production planning software package. And nothing improved!

When looking more thoroughly into the problem, the company dicovered that it was paying for having capacity reserved for its production. (The payments covered the hourly costs for the presses and the wages for the operators.) When the newspaper used the reserved capacity, it also paid for the paper, ink, and so on. However, when the same capacity, which often remained unused by the newspaper, was sold to external customers, these paid fully for the machine usage, wages, and materials. Therefore the company could claim payment from two sources for the same capacity.

As tempting as this strange arrangement was, the printing company often double-sold this reserved capacity, gambling that the newspaper would not use it. The deal between the printing company and the newspaper—and not the production planning—was the problem.

The Purpose and Applications of Flowcharts

Many of the problems that occur in organizations are connected to the business or work processes that are carried out there. Thus, as a first step in root cause analysis, making a flowchart of business processes is appropriate.

The main purpose of a flowchart is to portray the flow of activities in a process. As a first step in root cause analysis, flowcharts can be used to

- Map a process that illustrates where problems occur and which problems should be solved.

- Provide a basis for the ensuing root cause analysis by providing a detailed understanding of the process(es) that contain or influence the problem.

Problem solving

Root cause analysis

Problem understanding

Possible cause generation and consensus reaching

Problem and cause data collection

Possible cause analysis

Cause-and-effect analysis

Tool selection

Case Business Quality Travel

DIFFERENT TYPES OF FLOWCHARTS

Flowcharts come in many shapes and sizes. Some have been designed with special purposes in mind; others are simply variations that allow more or less information to be included within them. While this book does not pretend to cover flowcharting in detail, it is pertinent to mention some of the more useful types of flowcharts in terms of root cause analysis. These are:

- *Regular flowchart,* which simply depicts a sequence of activities or tasks and contains no other information.

- *Cross-functional flowchart,* which additionally indicates which person or department is responsible for each of the activities or tasks. This flowchart can also contain information on the duration of the activities, how much they cost, and so on.

- *Flowcharts on several levels,* which enable adding more detail to the charts. A simple flowchart usually forms the top-level chart, which gives a clear overview of the process. To provide information about certain steps in the process without clouding the top-level picture, each step is detailed in new charts on a level below. For very complex processes, there can be many such levels of charts.

Of these, we cover only the regular flowchart in this chapter.

The Steps in Using Flowcharts

1. Gather those working in the process to be documented in a meeting room with whiteboard facilities and plenty of adhesive notes in different colors.

2. Define the customers (internal or external) of the process, the output they receive, the input needed for the process, and the suppliers of that input.

3. Identify the main activities or tasks undertaken during the process to convert input to output.

4. Make adhesive notes in different colors to represent activities, products, documents, and other elements of the process.

5. Map the process by moving the notes around until they reflect the most realistic picture of the current process.

6. If there is a need to store the flowchart electronically, enter the chart into a computer.

AN EXAMPLE OF THE USE OF A FLOWCHART

A manufacturer of machines for paper mills had refined a design philosophy whereby almost 100% of the parts needed were purchased; the core competency of the company, therefore, was innovative designs, integration management, and assembly.

Many of these component parts were complex and could rarely be purchased on the spot. Rather, long-term agreements were often necessary and, in many cases, provided better deals. Other parts, like nuts and bolts, standard electric parts, and so forth, could be bought from almost any supplier able to deliver. During the last few months, many purchasing agents had left the company and were replaced by new ones. This led to many problems, such as higher prices for various parts, poor delivery performance of incoming parts, lower quality, and so forth.

Both to train new purchasers and to have a starting point for a closer analysis of these problems, a flowchart of the purchasing process was made. This process could be divided into five distinct phases, so the flowchart was made up of two levels. One covered the overall process while the next level contained more detailed maps of each of the five process segments. The overall chart and one of the detailed charts are shown on the next page.

Example Paper Mill Flowcharts

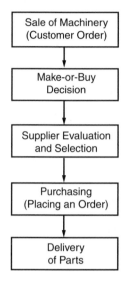

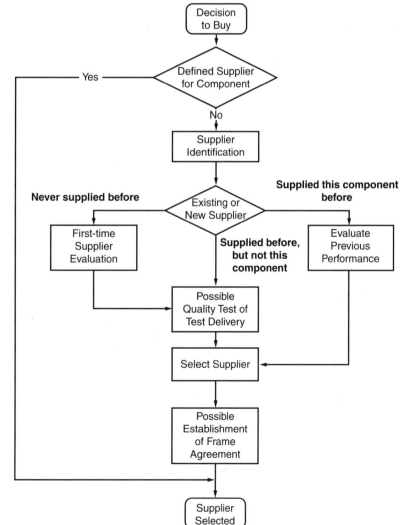

Problem
solving

Root cause
analysis

Problem
understanding

Possible cause
generation
and consensus
reaching

Problem and
cause
data collection

Possible cause
analysis

Cause-and-
effect
analysis

Tool selection

Case Business
Quality Travel

Checklist for Flowcharts

All (or at least a majority) of those working in the process to be flowcharted must be included in the activity. It is important to have all departments represented in the process included in the documentation task, both to ensure access to all necessary information and to create ownership of the end result. Furthermore, a supplier or customer, internal or external, may offer additional insight into the process.

❏ Perform an initial identification of the boundaries of the process, focusing on customers, output, input, and suppliers.

❏ Identify the main activities of the process that are carried out to convert the inputs to outputs.

❏ Represent all activities in the process—inputs, outputs, and so on—using adhesive notes in different colors.

❏ Move the adhesive notes around until they accurately depict the process being reviewed.

❏ If desired, add information to make the flowchart a cross-functional chart or a chart on several levels.

❏ When participants agree on the look of the flowchart, store the design into a computer (if there is a need for this).

❏ Use this flowchart as a picture of the process when applying other tools.

The Purpose and Applications of Critical Incident

When starting to solve a problem, many work simply from a gut feeling about what the problem really is. Finding the root cause of the problem, and ultimately its solution, would be easier if the true crux of the problem was acknowledged.

The main purpose of the critical incident method is to understand what *really* are the most troublesome symptoms in a problematic situation.

Root cause analysis helps you

- Understand which aspects of the problem need to be solved.
- Realize the nature of the problem and its consequences.

OPENNESS IS A PREREQUISITE

Most of the tools in root cause analysis have two things in common:

- They are best applied by a team of people working together to find the problem's causes and solve them.
- To work properly, they require an atmosphere of trust, openness, and honesty that encourages people to divulge important information without fearing consequences.

If this climate is not provided, chances are the root cause analysis will fail to bring to the surface the true nature of the problem or its causes. Creating this climate is everyone's responsibility, but management is clearly in a special situation, as they possess the most instruments for achieving this. This applies to all of the tools presented in this book, but it is pertinent especially with the critical incident method, as it can bring to light embarrassing situations.

The Steps in Using Critical Incident

1. Decide on the participants to be included, attempting to cover all departments or functional areas involved in the problem situation.

2. Ask each participant to answer in writing questions like: Which incident last week was most difficult to handle? Which episode created the biggest problems in terms of maintaining customer satisfaction? Which incident cost the most in terms of extra resources or direct expenditures?

3. Collect, sort, and analyze answers based on the frequency of different incidents.

4. Graphically present the sorted list to show the criticality of each incident.

5. Use the most critical incident(s) as a starting point for the search for problem causes.

AN EXAMPLE OF THE USE OF CRITICAL INCIDENT

Having grown considerably during the last two years, what once was a very small two-man management consulting firm had now become a successful outfit employing about 75 consultants. Since most of the problems the clients wanted solved were of a multidisciplinary nature, the company made it standard procedure to visit potential clients in pairs or even in threes.

Although no specific debate was ever started, there were some rumbles in the hallways and rumors going around that this sales technique was not very effective. Since no one was able to tell exactly what was wrong with it or what should be done differently, nothing happened to change it.

However, after a particularly frustrating visit to an important client, two of the consultants initiated a critical incident session to get to the bottom of the frustration. The consultants had themselves used the critical incident approach with clients many times and knew it well, but had never tried it internally. Nevertheless, it all went smoothly and generated some valuable insights.

The critical incident answers by one of the consultants are shown on the top of the next page, while a summary of the entire investigation is shown below it. It thus turned out that the real problem with the sales approach was that the consultants, making a living out of their credibility, often ended up looking silly, in disagreement, and generally feeling embarrassed in front of clients.

Example Sales Visits Critical Incident

> **Sales visits to clients: Critical incidents**
>
> - Suggesting a different solution than Thomas at SysCom.
>
> - Quoting an hourly rate at the meeting instead of in a written offer.
>
> - Being late for the meeting with ADA.
>
> - Showing up without having had time to prepare properly.

Type of incident	Frequency
Embarrassment by disagreeing with colleague	112
Being unprepared, thus giving a bad impression	39
Revealing too much information about prices or approaches	21
Losing a client to a competitor	14
Being late for meetings when the partner is already there	8
Being unable to suggest solutions to the client's problem	8
Feeling an obvious lack of chemistry with the client	5
Getting into an argument with the client	3
Spilling coffee on the client	1

Checklist for Critical Incident

❏ Assemble a group of participants for the critical incident session. The participants should represent all departments or functional areas of the company that are involved in or related to the problem situation.

❏ Ask each participant to individually write down answers to one or more predefined questions. The questions should cover issues related to the problem situation and which aspects cause the most problems, cost the most, generate most negative publicity, and so on.

❏ Collect the answers and sort according to frequency of mentioning; analyze for any patterns.

❏ Present the sorted list of incidents graphically, if necessary.

❏ Use the most critical incidents as a starting point for an ensuing search for causes to the problem.

The Purpose and Applications of Spider Charts

Flowcharts and critical incident aid in understanding the problem from an internal point of view. When seeking an external comparison, a spider chart can be a helpful tool.

The main purpose of the spider chart is to give a graphical impression of how the performance of business processes (or problem areas) compares with other organizations.

In root cause analysis, the main applications of a spider chart are to:

- Determine which problem is most critical.

- Compare the seriousness of problems and causes.

A SPIDER CHART IS A WAY OF BENCHMARKING

Benchmarking means comparing performance levels or practices with someone else, preferably someone with superior performance. Such comparison serves many purposes, including:

- Motivating improvement by proving that someone has solved a problem or reached higher levels of performance, thus showing that it is possible.

- Providing input as to what objectives should be set for the improvements stemming from problem solving and other improvement efforts.

- Learning how to do better by obtaining ideas and impulses from those who are better than yourself.

Furthermore, benchmarking against others can help you identify which areas of your operations need improvement and which are doing well already. This type of benchmarking can be facilitated by the use of a spider chart, as it allows comparing the performance levels of different processes or areas against others. Based on the results, the organization will get some direction as to where improvements are most needed.

Problem
solving

Root cause
analysis

Problem
understanding

Possible cause
generation
and consensus
reaching

Problem and
cause
data collection

Possible cause
analysis

Cause-and-
effect
analysis

Tool selection

Case Business
Quality Travel

The Steps in Using Spider Charts

1. Collect information needed to construct the spider chart—typically data from market analyses, surveys, competitor analyses, and so on.

2. Assign one variable to each spoke in the chart.

3. Divide each spoke into logical segments by using a separate unit of measurement for each variable. The farther from the center of the chart, the higher the performance.

4. Plot the performance data for each variable along the right spokes, using different colors or symbols to separate data points from those of different organizations.

5. Draw lines between the data points for each organization to generate performance profiles.

6. Identify the variables that show the largest gaps between your organization and the benchmarks.

AN EXAMPLE OF THE USE OF A SPIDER CHART

An average-sized social welfare office in a large city had a number of problems to cope with at any given time. One of the most serious of these was related to the security of the employees. The office had seen verbal abuse, physical assaults on case workers, unrest among waiting clients, and one instance of a serious stabbing of an employee.

The issue of employee safety had a number of different facets. Before trying to identify and remove the causes to any specific threats, it was necessary to rate which types of threats were most serious. Because matters of personal safety tend to make people think less rationally than when they face more neutral problems, it was unlikely that simply discussing the question among the employees would lead to a thorough understanding of the situation.

Because the state government regularly collected data on such problems from all offices in the state, comparing this office against others and state averages would be easy. Thus, office employees decided to construct a spider chart based on this data. The factors assigned to the spokes in the chart are listed on the top of the next page, while the chart is displayed below the list. From this chart, employees formed a clear picture as to which factors were especially severe when compared with the rest of the offices—namely, verbal abuse and threats, and serious property damage.

Example Social Welfare Office Spider Chart

Problem solving

Root cause analysis

Problem understanding

Possible cause generation and consensus reaching

Problem and cause data collection

Possible cause analysis

Cause-and-effect analysis

Tool selection

Case Business Quality Travel

Chart Categories (Frequency of Occurrence)

I.   Verbal abuse from clients
II.   Verbal threats by clients
III.   Minor physical abuse from clients
IV.   More serious physical abuse from clients
V.   Serious injuries inflicted by clients
VI.   Murders committed by clients
VII.   Minor property damage by clients
VIII. Serious property damage by clients

Problem
solving

Root cause
analysis

Problem
understanding

Possible cause
generation
and consensus
reaching

Problem and
cause
data collection

Possible cause
analysis

Cause-and-
effect
analysis

Tool selection

Case Business
Quality Travel

Checklist for Spider Charts

❏ Clearly define the problem or situation to be analyzed.

❏ Collect appropriate and relevant data before constructing the chart.

❏ Assign variables to the spokes in the chart.

❏ Divide the spokes into segments using a suitable unit of measurement for each variable.

❏ Plot the data for each variable and organization into the chart area.

❏ Using different colors or types of lines, draw lines between the data points for each organization to form performance profiles.

❏ Analyze the chart to identify the most significant gaps in relation to the benchmarks.

Spider Chart Template

Chart Categories

I.

II.

III.

IV.

V.

VI.

VII.

VIII.

Problem solving

Root cause analysis

Problem understanding

Possible cause generation and consensus reaching

Problem and cause data collection

Possible cause analysis

Cause-and-effect analysis

Tool selection

Case Business Quality Travel

The Purpose and Applications of Performance Matrices

When comparing different aspects in a spider chart, the focus is solely on the *performance* of the variables included in the chart. An equally relevant aspect to consider along with the current performance level, though, is the *importance* of each variable. The performance matrix is used to illustrate current performance *and* importance at the same time, helping to arrive at a sense of priority.

In root cause analysis, performance matrices can be used to illustrate problems or causes in terms of

- Which aspect of the problem is most important to attack.
- Which causes will give the most relief if removed.

FOUR QUADRANTS OF THE MATRIX

Factors being analyzed are placed in a matrix diagram. The area is divided into four sectors on the basis of current performance and importance of the factors.

The meaning of each quadrant is as follows:

- *Unimportant* (low importance, low performance): The performance level of this aspect of the problem is low, but the low importance renders it unnecessary to improve this particular issue.

- *Overkill* (low importance, high performance): The performance level of this aspect of the problem is high, but this is of less consequence because the issues in this quadrant are not especially important. Therefore, this is not a candidate for improvement.

- *Must be improved* (high importance, low performance): Factors that fall within this area are important, while the current performance level is low. As such, this is an obvious area for starting improvements.

- *OK* (high importance, high performance): A golden rule is that areas where the performance is already good should also be improved. However, factors that—in addition to being important—are not being performed well today (*must be improved*), should be improved first. If no factors fall within this quadrant, issues in the OK quadrant can be relevant candidates for improvement efforts.

The Steps in Using Performance Matrices

1. Construct an empty chart by placing **importance** on the horizontal axis and **current performance** on the vertical axis and dividing both axes into nine segments of equal size.

2. Use the performance matrix to decide which problems, factors, or issues to analyze.

3. Define a scale for each factor and divide it into nine, corresponding with the axes scales.

4. Place each factor in the chart according to its position along the two axes, using symbols to identify each factor.

5. Divide the chart into four quadrants approximately at the middle of each axis. If many factors are clustered in one area, place the division lines farther to one side.

6. Determine which factors fall within the quadrants.

AN EXAMPLE OF THE USE OF AN PERFORMANCE MATRIX

Because performance matrices are closely linked to spider charts, the example of the performance matrix is a follow-up to the previous example. From the spider chart, the social welfare office concluded that verbal abuse and threats and serious property damage were most prominent compared with other similar offices.

Because these conclusions focused on less serious damages to the employees, a performance matrix analysis was used as a supplement. The same factors were plotted in a matrix according to assessments of their performance and importance. (The completed matrix is shown on the following page.) The division lines between the quadrants were moved somewhat off center because some clusters were evident.

From this matrix, office workers concluded that the issue of serious property damage (category VIII) was still important. However, due to the much higher importance assessments of the physical damage factors to the employees compared with only verbal abuse, these four issues (categories III thru VI) were promoted at the expense of the verbal abuse and threats (categories I and II).

Problem solving

Root cause analysis

Problem understanding

Possible cause generation and consensus reaching

Problem and cause data collection

Possible cause analysis

Cause-and-effect analysis

Tool selection

Case Business Quality Travel

Problem
solving

Root cause
analysis

→ Problem
understanding

Possible cause
generation
and consensus
reaching

Problem and
cause
data collection

Possible cause
analysis

Cause-and-
effect
analysis

Tool selection

Case Business
Quality Travel

Example Social Welfare Office Performance Matrix

Chart Categories (Frequency of Occurrence)

I.   Verbal abuse from clients
II.   Verbal threats by clients
III.   Minor physical abuse from clients
IV.   More serious physical abuse from clients
V.   Serious injuries inflicted by clients
VI.   Murders committed by clients
VII.   Minor property damage by clients
VIII. Serious property damage by clients

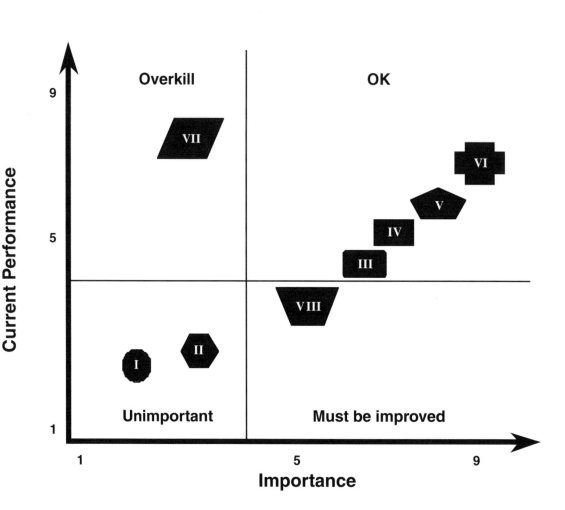

Checklist for Performance Matrices

A chart is first constructed with **importance** on the horizontal axis and **current performance** on the vertical, and with the axes divided into nine equal segments.

❑ Decide which factors will be analyzed.

❑ Agree on a logical scale for each factor and divide it into nine segments to allow plotting it into the empty chart.

❑ Plot all factors into the chart based on the assessments/measurements of their **importance** and **current performance**.

❑ Use different symbols to identify each factor when plotting the factors in the chart area.

❑ Divide the chart into quadrants. Draw the division lines from the center of each axis, skewing as needed if clusters are evident.

❑ Identify the factors within each quadrant, using the **must be improved** factors as a starting point for further actions.

Problem
solving

Root cause
analysis

Problem
understanding

Possible cause
generation
and consensus
reaching

Problem and
cause
data collection

Possible cause
analysis

Cause-and-
effect
analysis

Tool selection

Case Business
Quality Travel

Problem
solving

Root cause
analysis

Problem
understanding

Possible cause
generation
and consensus
reaching

Problem and
cause
data collection

Possible cause
analysis

Cause-and-
effect
analysis

Tool selection

Case Business
Quality Travel

Performance Matrix Template

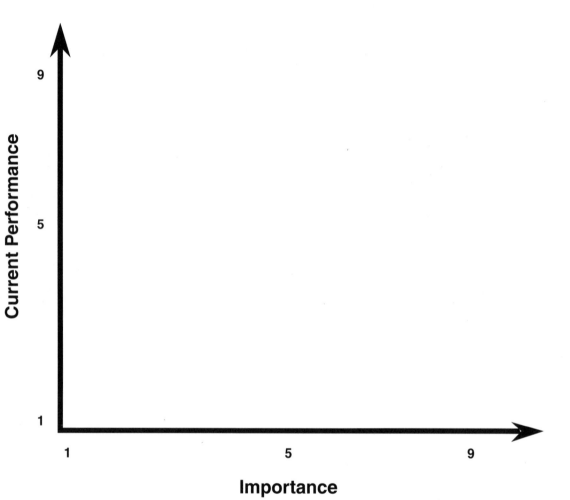

Problem Understanding Checklist

Although root cause analysis is not one clear process from start to finish, some distinctive stages in the analysis are discernible. This checklist helps assess whether the most important elements of the problem understanding stage have been accomplished before moving on.

❏ Agree on the problem to be attacked before embarking on the root cause analysis.

❏ Assess the situation in which the problem understanding will occur to select a suitable approach. Typical considerations are pre-analysis problem understanding, how many people have been involved in debates about the problem thus far, and so on.

❏ Choose among the following tools and approaches: flowchart, critical incident, spider chart, and performance matrix.

❏ Achieve a common understanding of the problem, its seriousness, and its consequences through use of the selected tools.

❏ Bring the problem understanding forward into the possible cause and consensus reaching stage.

Problem solving

Root cause analysis

Problem understanding

Possible cause generation and consensus reaching

Problem and cause data collection

Possible cause analysis

Cause-and-effect analysis

Tool selection

Case Business Quality Travel

Tools for Possible Cause Generation and Consensus Reaching

Chapter 4 presents idea-generating tools to help determine possible causes to a problem as well as tools the team can use to reach agreement in cases of disputes or differing views.

Possible Cause Generation and Consensus Reaching

Often a suspicion exists as to what causes the problem you are trying to solve. But, before you rush off to look further into it, consider other candidates. This is what possible cause generation is all about. Additionally, having an arsenal of tools to reach agreement when the team disagrees is important.

The tools available in this stage are

- Brainstorming

- Brainwriting

- Nominal group technique

- Paired comparisons

AVOID RUNNING OFF IN DIFFERENT DIRECTIONS

Five highly trained waiters on a cruise ship were given the task of finding out what caused long waiting lines during some meals and not during others. The team started capturing characteristics of meals resulting in queues, such as time of the week, the menu, the program for the day, and so on.

When deciding how to proceed, either by trying to vary these conditions to measure the effects or by conducting interviews with some guests, the team ran into a deadlock: three opted for the former approach, two for the latter. They never managed to set aside their differences and the team disbanded.

The Purpose and Applications of Brainstorming

The problems we face in our work life rarely have one easily identifiable cause. Finding their root cause requires **creativity**!

Brainstorming is a great way to generate as many good ideas as possible related to a given subject. Its purpose is to

- Generate a list of problem areas that can be improved.

- Identify possible consequences stemming from the problem being analyzed.

- Generate a list of possible areas that constitute causes to the problem.

- Encourage thinking about ways to eliminate the causes.

TWO TYPES OF BRAINSTORMING

In root cause analysis, brainstorming is not one single, well-defined activity. Actually, there are two different ways to brainstorm.

- *Structured brainstorming,* where each participant in turn launches one idea, is more structured and ensures equal participation, but is less spontaneous and to some extent limits the possibility for building on one another's ideas. This type of approach is called round-robin brainstorming.

- *Unstructured brainstorming,* where everyone can freely launch ideas, is very spontaneous, but is often more confusing and can lead to one or more persons dominating the activity. The opportunities for piggybacking ideas are also better in this version, which is sometimes also called free-wheeling brainstorming.

Except for these differences in the order by which ideas are launched, the two approaches are identical; the steps for applying them are presented on the next page.

Problem solving

Root cause analysis

Problem understanding

Possible cause generation and consensus reaching

Problem and cause data collection

Possible cause analysis

Cause-and-effect analysis

Tool selection

Case Business Quality Travel

The Steps in Brainstorming

1. Clearly define the topic to brainstorm and write it on top of a whiteboard or a flip chart.

2. Allow participants to launch ideas according to the approach used, structured or unstructured.

3. Write down every idea launched, using the same wording as the original proposition.

4. Do not discuss, criticize, or evaluate ideas during the session.

5. Allow the flow of ideas to stagnate once, because it will usually pick up again. Close the process when new ideas are only reformulations of previously launched ideas or when fewer new ideas are evident.

6. Evaluate the ideas by sorting them into groups, either by theme or by decreasing potential.

AN EXAMPLE OF THE USE OF BRAINSTORMING

When many of the receptionists at a large international business hotel realized that it frequently took more time to check their guests in and out than what had been set aside, they initiated a brainstorming session to identify the reasons. One of the managers of the hotel was a member of a group from the hotel chain administration who frequently traveled to many hotels to evaluate their service, and could confirm the considerably lower performance. He and seven receptionists formed the brainstorming team.

They defined the theme of the brainstorming as "reasons we make our guests wait unnecessarily long when checking in and out of our hotel." The free-wheeling approach was chosen, and the group started its session an hour before lunch on a Thursday. A group clerk took the stand by the whiteboard, and the brainstorming went on for about 50 minutes. By that time, 42 ideas had been tabled, though some were closely related or similar. After a break for lunch, the team combined and grouped ideas, eventually sorting them according to their impact on the problem.

Some important ideas that resulted from the brainstorming included: the registration form required more information than was necessary from the guests; the hotel lacked a guest database that could retrieve information for repeat customers; the desk was understaffed during peak hours; the desk staff was required to handle queries about directions, transportation, and so forth; and there were too few credit card company links. Needless to say, these had to be further analyzed, but they represented a very good starting point for the ensuing improvement efforts.

Checklist for Brainstorming

Before the actual brainstorming starts, clearly define and communicate to everyone the topic of the session.

❑ Decide which mode of idea launching to use, free-wheeling or round-robin.

❑ Record ideas as they are launched; do not attempt to reformulate or redefine them.

❑ Allow everyone the opportunity (and time) to launch all their ideas.

❑ Do not allow criticism during the idea-generation phase.

❑ Allow the flow of ideas to slow once, then to resume, without terminating the session.

❑ Stop the session when the flow of ideas slows again or new ideas are variants of previously launched concepts.

❑ Evaluate (and possibly reformulate) the ideas.

❑ Combine and group ideas.

❑ If the brainstorming is part of a larger project or process, agree on clear tasks with responsibilities and deadlines to further process the outcome of the brainstorming.

Problem solving

Root cause analysis

Problem understanding

Possible cause generation and consensus reaching

Problem and cause data collection

Possible cause analysis

Cause-and-effect analysis

Tool selection

Case Business Quality Travel

Brainstorming Recording Template

Problem solving

Root cause analysis

Problem understanding

Possible cause generation and consensus reaching

Problem and cause data collection

Possible cause analysis

Cause-and-effect analysis

Tool selection

Case Business Quality Travel

Brainstorming

Topic:

Participants: Date:

Ideas

Idea Groups

The Purpose and Applications of Brainwriting

While brainwriting serves the same purpose as brainstorming, it offers these advantages:

- Everyone has better access to the process.

- Participants can describe more detailed and coherent ideas.

- It is possible to protect the anonymity of the participants, which is useful if you're dealing with a touchy subject.

Typical application during root cause analysis includes generating ideas about problems, consequences, and ways to eliminate the causes in situations where

- complex ideas are expected, or

- it is feared that some people might dominate the brainstorming were it conducted orally.

TWO TYPES OF BRAINWRITING

There are two ways to conduct a brainwriting session. The objective is the same with both approaches and most of the steps are identical, the difference lies in the way ideas are recorded.

- In the card method, ideas are written on small cards and circulated among the participants who add related ideas or expand on the existing ones.

- In the gallery method, ideas are written on a number of whiteboards or flip charts and the participants circulate among these to add related ideas or expand on the existing ones.

Problem solving

Root cause analysis

Problem understanding

Possible cause generation and consensus reaching

Problem and cause data collection

Possible cause analysis

Cause-and-effect analysis

Tool selection

Case Business Quality Travel

The Steps in Brainwriting

1. As with brainstorming, start by clearly defining the target topic for possible cause generation. Depending on the method used, write the topic

   • On a whiteboard in the gallery method.

   • On participants' individual cards in the card method.

2. Have participants write down their ideas on their cards or on the whiteboard. Encourage precise formulations.

3. Allow participants to add to others' ideas to reap effects from combining ideas or further developing them.

4. Ask the group to discuss the ideas and, if possible, sort them into classes.

AN EXAMPLE OF THE USE OF BRAINWRITING

At the hotel described in the brainstorming example, the team that looked at why checking in and out took so long came up with a multitude of possible reasons. Many of these involved more extensive issues than could possibly be changed by the receptionists, either because they involved large investments or affected the policy and operations of other parts of the hotel.

To take the ideas further and look at possible ways to remedy the situation, a different group was formed. When three receptionists, the general manager, the accountant, and a computer analyst tried to build on the success from the previous brainstorming by using the same approach, the once-creative receptionists seemed repressed and contributed few ideas. It was also apparent that the sole reason behind this change in behavior was the dominating presence of the general manager. The group therefore discarded what had been done during the fruitless brainstorming session and instead conducted a round of brainwriting.

Even though this did not immediately restore the previous creativity of the receptionists, the result was far better. Some good ideas centered around installing a simple guest database that would give quick responses when searching for a guest's name, encouraging guests to settle their bills the previous night to allow express check-out in the morning, rethinking the manpower use throughout the day to better cover the peaks, and placing an "oracle" in the reception area to answer questions not related directly to the rooms or accounts.

Checklist for Brainwriting

Before the brainwriting starts, clearly define and communicate to everyone the topic of the session.

❏ Decide which approach to use, the gallery or the card method.

❏ Have the individual participants generate and write down ideas.

❏ When everyone has completed the idea launching, have the group try to build on one another's ideas and combine and extend them.

❏ Evaluate (and possibly reformulate) the ideas.

❏ Combine and group ideas.

❏ If the brainwriting is part of a larger project or process, agree on clear tasks with responsibilities and deadlines to further process the outcome of the brainwriting.

Problem solving

Root cause analysis

Problem understanding

Possible cause generation and consensus reaching

Problem and cause data collection

Possible cause analysis

Cause-and-effect analysis

Tool selection

Case Business Quality Travel

Brainwriting Card and Whiteboard Template

Brainwriting

Topic: Date:

Individual Ideas

Brainwriting

Topic: Date:

Group Ideas

The Purpose and Applications of Nominal Group Technique (NGT)

When brainstorming, the loudest person or persons can sometimes dominate the activity. While discussing ideas, these people will generally continue to dominate, which can cause the group to arrive at minority decisions.

The nominal group technique can facilitate a form of brainstorming in which all participants have the same vote when selecting solutions.

Typical root cause analysis applications are

- Generating ideas by tapping the entire group's potential.

- Gaining consensus about which ideas to pursue further throughout the analysis.

WHAT IS CONSENSUS?

Consensus is a somewhat tricky concept that is often believed to mean that absolutely everyone involved in a decision must agree if it is to be a consensus decision. Fortunately, this is not the case. According to Webster's dictionary, consensus means "The judgment arrived at by most of those concerned."

Obtaining full agreement from every person in a group is impossible, so only a majority of those with a vote in the matter agree. This makes life much simpler when regarding root cause analysis, which is based on a joint undertaking by a group and involves creativity and decisions along the way.

When the group votes on an issue and the majority favors one option, consensus has been achieved and the group can move on. If the rules of consensus have been made clear to the group at the outset, such majority decisions should cause no tension, as everyone knows they must be abided by.

Problem solving

Root cause analysis

Problem understanding

Possible cause generation and consensus reaching

Problem and cause data collection

Possible cause analysis

Cause-and-effect analysis

Tool selection

Case Business Quality Travel

Problem
solving

Root cause
analysis

Problem
understanding

Possible cause
generation
and consensus
reaching

Problem and
cause
data collection

Possible cause
analysis

Cause-and-
effect
analysis

Tool selection

Case Business
Quality Travel

The Steps in Nominal Group Technique

1. Each person generates ideas and writes them on **idea cards**, one idea on each card.

2. The session leader assigns each idea a letter (from A onward) and registers it on a flip chart. Participants briefly discuss ideas for clarification and elimination of similar ideas.

3. Participants individually rank the ideas on their ranking card by selecting up to five ideas and assigning points to them, from 5 for the most important/best idea down to 1 for the least important/good idea.

4. The session leader collects the ranking cards, and totals the points.

5. The idea achieving the highest total score is the group's prioritized idea or solution, and will be the logical starting point for the ensuing activities in the root cause analysis.

AN EXAMPLE OF THE USE OF THE NOMINAL GROUP TECHNIQUE

A medium-sized high school faced some severe problems with bullying and generally unacceptable behavior, though not only among the students. During the last few years, a number of skilled teachers had left the school due to the poor work climate among the employees. A task force of five teachers, two students, one custodial worker, and one administrator was assembled to look into the problems.

The team soon discovered that there were immense differences in opinion as to what caused the low job satisfaction, and the different *groups* of people tended to blame the others. After a few weeks of fruitless discussions, the task force was no closer to solving the problems, let alone agreeing on their causes. To move the job forward, they agreed to try the nominal group technique.

There was no lack of ideas for possible causes and these had been recorded in minutes from the meetings held so far. These were defined to be the set to vote on, and a list with assigned letters was produced, as shown on the top of the following page. Below the idea list, one teacher's ranking card is depicted. Finally, the resulting total scores for the different ideas are shown at the bottom of the page. From this exercise, the task force was able to move on, concentrating on the four highest ranked consensus ideas: 1. the isolation of the job, 2. time pressures, 3. the lack of activities of a social nature, and 4. the appearance of the school building and facilities.

Example High School Nominal Group Technique

A	People simply do not know one another
B	There are no social arrangements
C	People don't care about other people
D	The staff takes after the students, but makes everything more serious
E	The school looks so sloppy, there are no incentives for behaving any better
F	Too much work and too little time to do it
G	The teachers look down at the other employees
H	Manners are a neglected subject
I	Everyone works alone; there are no tasks requiring a collective effort
J	Too many aggressive young males
K	Competition for pay raises fosters a cold atmosphere

Ranking Card NGT

Problem: Bad work climate in school

Idea	Points
F	5
K	4
I	1
A	2
D	3

Nominal Group Technique

Problem: Bad work climate in school

Idea	Points	Total
A	2 3 1	6
B	4 5 1 2	12
C	1 1 5	7
D	2 2 3 1	8
E	4 4 3	11
F	5 5 4 5 1	20
G	2 3	5
H	2 3	5
I	5 5 4 3 4	21
J	1 2	3
K	3 4	7

Problem solving

Root cause analysis

Problem understanding

Possible cause generation and consensus reaching

Problem and cause data collection

Possible cause analysis

Cause-and-effect analysis

Tool selection

Case Business Quality Travel

Checklist for Nominal Group Technique

Before the possible cause generation is started, clearly define and communicate to everyone the topic of the session.

❑ Select a session leader.

❑ Distribute idea cards to participants.

❑ Individual participants generate ideas and write them down on their idea cards.

❑ When everyone has completed the idea production, write the ideas on a whiteboard or flip chart and assign each a letter.

❑ Discuss ideas to clarify vague entries and eliminate similar ones.

❑ Have the participants individually and without any influence from others rank the ideas that appeal most to them using their ranking cards.

❑ Have the session leader collect the cards and total the scores for all ideas.

❑ Accept the highest-ranking ideas as the group's consensus solution.

Nominal Group Technique Idea and Ranking Cards

Ranking Card NGT	
Problem:	
Idea	Points

Nominal Group Technique		
Problem:		
Idea	Points	Total
A		
B		
C		
D		
E		
F		
G		
H		
I		
J		
K		

Problem
solving

Root cause
analysis

Problem
understanding

Possible cause
generation
and consensus
reaching

Problem and
cause
data collection

Possible cause
analysis

Cause-and-
effect
analysis

Tool selection

Case Business
Quality Travel

The Purpose and Applications of Paired Comparisons

The ideas available for voting on might be many and the ideas may vary. In such situations, it can be difficult to decide which idea to vote for, and the results might be determined by coincidence.

Like the other methods described in this chapter, paired comparisons aim at prioritization and consensus reaching, but does so through a sequence of paired comparisons. Single decisions are easier to make than selecting among a large number of possible solutions.

Typical applications of paired comparisons include:

• Prioritizing among different alternative problems or causes

• Helping decisions surface when there are many alternatives

METHODS SIMILAR TO PAIRED COMPARISONS

There are other methods that also rely on the basic idea of prioritizing among two or more ideas or elements to end up with a ranked list. While these might work just as well as paired comparisons or the nominal group technique, they are often more complex without necessarily adding benefits. Some such methods you might want to consider are

• Balance sheet: a simple tool where pros and cons of the alternative ideas are listed in an effort to clarify what each entails

• Criteria rating form (sometimes called criteria testing): a numerical approach for applying certain evaluation criteria to a set of ideas to choose among them

• Weighted voting: a technique similar to the nominal group technique

The Steps in Paired Comparisons

1. Clearly identify the alternatives to be compared. The total number, denoted N, should be manageable, that is, not more than eight.

2. Make a matrix with the alternatives, coded by letters, as row headings and the pairs as column headings, indicated by letters only to save space. The number of pairs, P, is determined by the following formula:

$$P = \frac{[N \times (N-1)]}{2}.$$

3. Column by column, each participant votes for one of the alternatives; the votes are logged in the matrix.

4. After participants have voted for all pairs, sum the total number for each pair; this should equal the number of participants.

5. Sum the number of votes given for each alternative to give the row totals. The highest scoring alternative is the preferred one according to the group.

AN EXAMPLE OF THE USE OF PAIRED COMPARISONS

A large car dealer had been in the same perfect downtown location, in terms of customer availability, for years. This particular location also generated problems, though, especially for the repair shop. Having very little space available, it was difficult to park cars that were waiting to be serviced or picked up. Customers often waited up to an hour to get their cars out from the lot.

Although it would be impossible to do something about the size of the space, the two foremen and five mechanics put their heads together to look into the dominating reasons why customers were kept waiting. After brainstorming among themselves and soliciting ideas from their coworkers, they sized the list down to the one shown on the following page.

However, when trying to decide which of these were contributing most to the problem, thus prioritizing which to attack first, major disagreements surfaced. Following heated debate, on the verge of developing into a physical fight, the manager of the dealership suggested they use paired comparisons to arrive at a conclusion.

The mechanics designed the matrix on their whiteboard and went through the entire voting procedure, as shown at the lower half of the next page. Working from this, they implemented a system where magnetic boxes containing the key were attached to the roof of each car in the parking lot. The boxes could be removed only by using a remote control, which every mechanic was furnished, ensuring that whenever a car had to be moved, the keys were readily available to do so.

Example Car Dealer Paired Comparisons

Problem solving

Root cause analysis

Problem understanding

→ Possible cause generation and consensus reaching

Problem and cause data collection

Possible cause analysis

Cause-and-effect analysis

Tool selection

Case Business Quality Travel

A	No system for parking cars in the order in which they will be collected
B	Some people park in a way that requires much more space than necessary
C	Whenever a car is to be moved, the keys are impossible to find
D	The gate from the lot to the repair shop is too narrow
E	Too many cars are accepted each day, resulting in some of them having to stay parked overnight

	A/B	A/C	A/D	A/E	B/C	B/D	B/E	C/D	C/E	D/E	Total
A	5	2	3	3							13
B	2				1	4	5				12
C		5			6			6	5		22
D			4			3		1		4	12
E				4			2		2	3	11
Number of votes	7	7	7	7	7	7	7	7	7	7	

Checklist for Paired Comparisons

Before the paired comparison starts, generate a list of alternatives—for example, through brainstorming or brainwriting.

❑ Reduce the number of alternatives to an amount that can be practically handled in the comparison session, that is, not more than eight.

❑ Determine the number of pairs and design a matrix.

❑ Have each participant vote for the pairs, column by column in the matrix; log the votes.

❑ Control the number of votes cast by summing the total number of votes for each pair.

❑ In case of discrepancies in the number of votes, revote the pairs in dispute.

❑ Sum the grand totals for each alternative.

❑ The alternative receiving the highest number of votes is declared the consensus decision.

Paired Comparisons Template

Problem solving

Root cause analysis

Problem understanding

→ Possible cause generation and consensus reaching

Problem and cause data collection

Possible cause analysis

Cause-and-effect analysis

Tool selection

Case Business Quality Travel

	A/B	A/C	A/D	A/E	A/F	B/C	B/D	B/E	B/F	C/D	C/E	C/F	D/E	D/F	E/F	Total
A	☐	☐	☐	☐	☐											☐
B	☐					☐	☐	☐	☐							☐
C		☐				☐				☐	☐	☐				☐
D			☐				☐			☐			☐	☐		☐
E				☐				☐			☐		☐		☐	☐
F					☐				☐			☐		☐	☐	☐
Number of votes																

Possible Cause Generation and Consensus Reaching Checklist

Although root cause analysis is not one clear process from start to finish, some distinctive stages in the analysis are discernible. This checklist helps assess whether the most important elements of the possible cause generation and consensus reaching stage have been accomplished before moving on.

❏ Decide which problem needs possible cause generation and clearly define the objective of the session. Typical applications include generating ideas about which problem to solve, possible causes for a problem, and possible solutions to a problem.

❏ Assess the situation in which the possible cause generation will take place to select a suitable approach. Typical considerations include allowing everyone to participate properly, anonymity, complexity, and so on. Tools to choose between are brainstorming and brainwriting.

❏ After the generation is completed, decide if prioritization of the generated ideas is necessary. If so, assess whether this could be accomplished by analyzing the entire set of ideas. The purpose of this assessment is to select between nominal group technique or paired comparisons.

❏ Reach a consensus of the prioritization of the ideas by using one of these techniques. The consensus solution is taken into the possible cause and data collection stage.

Problem solving

Root cause analysis

Problem understanding

Possible cause generation and consensus reaching

Problem and cause data collection

Possible cause analysis

Cause-and-effect analysis

Tool selection

Case Business Quality Travel

Tools for Possible Cause and Data Collection

This chapter contains a selection of tools and techniques that you can use to collect data in the root cause analysis. Typically, these tools and techniques are used in conjunction with many of the other tools in this book.

Problem and Cause Data Collection

One important distinction between haphazard problem solving and structured root cause analysis is the extent to which data are collected and used. While the former tends to result in "shots in the dark," analysis based on insight and facts has a much better chance of accomplishing its objectives.

Thus, systematic collection of valid and reliable data is an important activity in root cause analysis.

The tools that can be used for this purpose are

- Sampling
- Surveys
- Check sheet

COLLECT A REPRESENTATIVE SET OF DATA

After receiving a complaint letter from a customer, the manager of a small restaurant changed both the menu and the practice that allowed guests to reserve tables. The complaining customer wanted a wider selection of appetizers, main courses, and desserts, and did not like the fact that when he visited the restaurant, there often were no tables available.

After having made changes according to this customer's wishes, the business gradually declined. People who previously dined there several times a week and now only came by occasionally were highly displeased with the changes that had been made. Had the proprietor collected a representative set of data earlier, instead of acting on the single complaint, the costly experience could have been avoided.

The Purpose and Applications of Sampling

During the root cause analysis, it is often necessary to collect data about the problem and its possible causes. Collecting data might take a long time, be costly, or require a lot of effort. Sampling is a way of economizing the data-collection process.

The main purpose of sampling is to draw conclusions about a larger group based on a smaller sample, as long as you are aware of the sample's limitations.

Applications in root cause analysis include:

- Effectively collecting data about problems or causes

- Gaining a better understanding of the situation

Problem solving

Root cause analysis

Problem understanding

Possible cause generation and consensus reaching

Problem and cause data collection

Possible cause analysis

Cause-and-effect analysis

Tool selection

Case Business Quality Travel

TYPES OF SAMPLING

Sampling is a collective term that encompasses several approaches to the cost- and time-efficient collection of data. Some of the most common types of sampling include:

- *Random sampling:* where random numbers are used to determine which units will be drawn from the larger population. Random numbers can be found in special tables, by using a computer to generate the numbers, or simply by throwing dice. An example is pulling out numbers 4, 11, 19, 21, 34, and so on, for testing for defects.

- *Systematic sampling:* a means to overcome the fact that random sampling can at times be difficult or even impossible. In systematic sampling, measures are made at fixed intervals of time, numbers, length, and so on. For instance, every 20 minutes the number of customers waiting in line are counted.

- *Stratified sampling:* a necessary tool when you know that there are differences between categories within the entire population. In such situations, data is purposely collected from each of the categories so that the samples represent the categories in the right proportions to one another. If a company has seven salespeople, customer satisfaction scores can be collected from the customers of each, relative to the number of customers each serves.

- *Cluster sampling:* an adequate approach when the population is known to be stable and without much variation. In this case, a group of the units is taken to represent the whole population—for example, the entire batch of parts produced during an hour to represent the entire week's production.

Problem
solving

Root cause
analysis

Problem
understanding

Possible cause
generation
and consensus
reaching

Problem and
cause
data collection

Possible cause
analysis

Cause-and-
effect
analysis

Tool selection

Case Business
Quality Travel

The Steps in Using Sampling

Unlike most of the other tools presented here, sampling is not one unified tool where the steps can easily be outlined. Rather, sampling is used to support other tools. Some important issues to keep in mind include:

- Assess the nature of the population to be sampled to decide on a suitable type of sampling approach (take into account the homogeneity of the population, any clustering of data, and so on).

- Collect the sample of data according to the chosen sampling approach.

- By calculating simple figures such as averages, means, and so on, you can test whether the sample is a reasonable representation of the population.

AN EXAMPLE OF THE USE OF SAMPLING

Customers of a manufacturer of ballpoint pens used for promotions frequently complained because many of the pens didn't work or stopped working after a relatively short time. The pens' recipients transferred the same level of quality to the customers' companies.

The pens were manufactured in seven different manufacturing lines. To determine if the quality varied among these lines, the company wanted to undertake a random quality-control assessment of the finished products. However, to ensure that the same data was collected from all seven lines, the company needed to introduce a systematic sampling procedure: for one week, they collected the first three pens produced each hour from each of the seven lines. Each pen was tested immediately and again after having been used for one minute.

The data showed clear differences between the manufacturing lines. Five lines produced pens of adequate quality, while two others generated close to 95 percent of the defective product. After these stunning results, the next step was to start looking for the causes for these high defect rates, which is a different story.

Checklist for Sampling

❑ Before sampling, assess the sample population to ensure that a suitable sampling method is being used.

❑ During the sampling, collect data in accordance with the chosen sampling approach.

❑ After some time of sampling, ensure that the sample does in fact represent an accurate picture of the entire population.

A FEW WORDS ON SAMPLE SIZE

Even after deciding on a type of sampling, you still need to answer two important questions.

- How many samples need to be collected?

- What is the size of the samples?

There is no simple way to answer these two questions, but there are some factors that impact the decisions, including:

- Whether the collected data will be discrete—that is, correct/wrong, yes/no, and so on—or continuous—that is, measurable in inches, pounds, volts, and so on

- The size of the total population

- How difficult it will be to collect data

- How costly it will be to collect data

- The expected level of variation in the sampled population

- What the consequences of inaccurate samples could be

After using sampling techniques a few times, gut feeling or intuition is often the most important determinant.

This brief discussion in no way exhausts the topic of sampling, but should give you a basic insight into the technique. The purpose of sampling is to be able to collect a smaller amount of data and have it viewed as representative for the entire data population.

Problem solving

Root cause analysis

Problem understanding

Possible cause generation and consensus reaching

Problem and cause data collection

Possible cause analysis

Cause-and-effect analysis

Tool selection

Case Business Quality Travel

The Purpose and Applications of Surveys

The data mentioned in the example of sampling were quantitative and easily measured. When you want to collect data about people's attitudes, feelings, or opinions, an additional instrument is useful, namely a survey. Surveys are helpful when collecting such data.

The main purpose of surveys is to collect data from respondents.

In root cause analysis, the most common uses of surveys include:

- Collecting customer satisfaction data related to a problem

- Determining customer needs and expectations

WAYS TO CONDUCT SURVEYS

First, a survey is a structured data collection session that requires a predefined set of questions. These questions are normally contained in a questionnaire developed for the survey.

Second, there are at least two different ways to solicit answers to the questions from the respondents in the survey, including:

- Having the respondents complete the questionnaire in writing.

- Conducting an interview with the respondent and letting the interviewer fill in the answers. Such interviews can be performed over the phone or through personal contact.

For all surveys, large amounts of data can be collected relatively easily and inexpensively. While questionnaires filled in by the respondents generate the most data per dollar, interviews tend to give data of higher quality.

The Steps in Using Surveys

1. Clearly define the objective of the survey and how the data will be used later.

2. Determine what information is required to achieve this objective.

3. Decide how the survey will be undertaken—that is, written (via mail, fax, e-mail, or the Internet) or verbal (by telephone or in person).

4. Develop the questionnaire, keeping in mind issues such as type and sequence of questions, understandability, language, grouping of questions, brevity, and so on.

5. Test the questionnaire to ensure that all questions are easy to understand, and can measure what they are intended to.

6. Identify the sample of respondents.

7. Perform the survey according to the chosen approach.

AN EXAMPLE OF THE USE OF A SURVEY

A computer store had specialized in selling to first-time unskilled buyers, some of whom were touching a computer for the first time. Many of the customers required a lot of support and technical guidance during the first few weeks after the purchase, and many customers complained about their buying experience.

To determine what caused these problems, the store developed a customer satisfaction survey; they sent a simple questionnaire (shown on the following page) to every buyer six weeks after the purchase, along with a return envelope with prepaid postage. To encourage people to return the questionnaire, a drawing for $1000 in software was held after four months.

The survey yielded about 150 completed questionnaires. After company officials asassembled and analyzed the data, the cause of most dissatisfaction became clear.

Problem solving

Root cause analysis

Problem understanding

Possible cause generation and consensus reaching

Problem and cause data collection

Possible cause analysis

Cause-and-effect analysis

Tool selection

Case Business Quality Travel

Problem
solving

Root cause
analysis

Problem
understanding

Possible cause
generation
and consensus
reaching

Problem and
cause
data collection

Possible cause
analysis

Cause-and-
effect
analysis

Tool selection

Case Business
Quality Travel

Example Computer Store Customer Satisfaction Survey

Customer Satisfaction Survey

To improve our service to you, we are conducting this survey to rate your experience in buying a computer from us. We appreciate your taking time to complete the questionnaire.

Please indicate your responses by checking the appropriate boxes.

	Poor				Excellent	
	1	2	3	4	5	6
1. Overall, how would you rate your purchase from our store?	❑	❑	❑	❑	❑	❑

2. How would you rate the folllowing aspects of our service:

	1	2	3	4	5	6
Computer hardware and accessories selection?	❑	❑	❑	❑	❑	❑
Hardware and accessories prices?	❑	❑	❑	❑	❑	❑
Software selection?	❑	❑	❑	❑	❑	❑
Software prices?	❑	❑	❑	❑	❑	❑
Salesperson's knowledge and ability to help you?	❑	❑	❑	❑	❑	❑
Delivery time of the equipment you bought?	❑	❑	❑	❑	❑	❑
Quality of the instructions and manual?	❑	❑	❑	❑	❑	❑
Technical support during installation?	❑	❑	❑	❑	❑	❑
Technical support after installation?	❑	❑	❑	❑	❑	❑
Reliability of the equipment?	❑	❑	❑	❑	❑	❑

3. Would you recommend our store to others?   ❑ Yes   ❑ No

4. What is your age?   ❑ <30   ❑ >30

5. What is your gender?   ❑ Male   ❑ Female

Thank You Very Much!

Checklist for Surveys

The **objective** of the survey must be clearly identified before preparing the survey.

❏ Identify the type and amount of data required.

❏ Evaluate possible survey methods and select a suitable approach.

❏ Consider how the collected data will be analyzed, keeping in mind which analysis tools will be used.

❏ Design the questionnaire so the layout fits the objective of the survey, the data to be collected, and the analysis approach selected.

❏ Pretest the questionnaire internally before using it, to adjust and improve both the structure and the questions.

❏ Identify the sample of survey respondents.

❏ Conduct the survey according to the selected approach.

❏ Analyze the collected data using the defined analysis methods.

Problem solving

Root cause analysis

Problem understanding

Possible cause generation and consensus reaching

Problem and cause data collection

Possible cause analysis

Cause-and-effect analysis

Tool selection

Case Business Quality Travel

Problem
solving

Root cause
analysis

Problem
understanding

Possible cause
generation
and consensus
reaching

▶ Problem and
cause
data collection

Possible cause
analysis

Cause-and-
effect
analysis

Tool selection

Case Business
Quality Travel

The Purpose and Applications of Check Sheets

Data collection can often become an unstructured and messy exercise. A check sheet is a table or a form used to systematically register data as it is collected.

The main purpose of a check sheet is to ensure that all data is registered correctly.

Main applications include:

- Registering how often different problems occur

- Registering the frequency of incidents that are believed to cause problems

---

WHAT DATA IS NEEDED IN ROOT CAUSE ANALYSIS?

Data is a word that sounds very formal—"data is used by bureaucratic governmental institutions and by computers; in the practical world of root cause analysis and problem solving, there is no need for data."

This is the view of many people working with root cause analysis. However, one simple definition of the *data* is:

"A collection of facts from which conclusions may be drawn."

Isn't this exactly what we need in root cause analysis? As you will see throughout this book, a multitude of different input is essential for a good analysis. This input is called *data,* and it takes many shapes and forms.

Typical types of data that are used in root cause analysis include:

- Events that occur

- The frequency of events

- Errors or defects discovered in products

- How long different tasks take to perform

- The costs of certain aspects of a process

The Steps in Using Check Sheets

1. Clearly define what events are to be recorded. (Add a category of "other" to capture incidents not easily categorized into any of the specified groups.)

2. Define the period for data recording and suitable intervals.

3. Design the check sheet to be used during data recording, allocating space for recording each event, and for summarizing within the intervals and the entire recording period.

4. Perform the data collection during the agreed period, ensuring that everyone understands the tasks and events to be recorded.

5. Analyze the data to identify events with unusually high or low occurrences.

Problem solving

Root cause analysis

Problem understanding

Possible cause generation and consensus reaching

Problem and cause data collection

Possible cause analysis

Cause-and-effect analysis

Tool selection

Case Business Quality Travel

AN EXAMPLE OF THE USE OF A CHECK SHEET

A bookstore located in a large shopping mall consistently achieved lower sales per day than budgeted. The staff noticed that quite a few customers came into the store to browse, but left without buying anything. When considering this problem (not tapping the customer base potential there), a wide range of possible causes surfaced including:

- The customers did not find what they were looking for.

- The staff did not offer the necessary help.

- Sought items were temporarily sold out.

- Sought items were not carried by the store.

- Prices were too high.

- There was too long a line at the checkout counter.

- Certain types of credit cards were not accepted.

- Lighting was poor in some areas of the store.

- There were no places to sit and look through books before deciding to buy.

The difficulty of identifying the actual problem and how often it occurred made it difficult for the store personnel to implement any changes. Thus, during a two-week period, many of the customers leaving without making any purchases were courteously asked why this happened. The responses were logged in a check sheet, shown on the following page, and give a much clearer idea of where to start to improve the situation.

Example Bookstore Check Sheet

Cause of no purchase	Week 1	Week 2	Total number of occurrences per cause
Could not find item	卌 卌 卌 II	卌 卌 卌 卌	37
No offer of help	卌 卌 IIII	卌 I	20
Item sold out	II	III	5
Item not carried	III	卌 I	9
Prices too high	I		1
Line too long	I	III	4
Wrong credit cards	II		2
Poor lighting	卌 II	卌 卌 II	19
No place to sit	II	IIII	6
Total number of causes per week	49	54	103

DO NOT LET THE CHECK SHEET MAKE YOU
OVERLOOK CAUSES

When recommending the use of check sheets during data collection in root cause analysis, a word of warning is appropriate. If the categories of events you are recording in the data collection period have been meticulously defined and inserted into the check sheet, other significant occurrences might often be overlooked.

One way of reducing the risk of making this mistake is to add a category termed "other," in which you can place everything that seems prudent to record but does not fit into one of the other categories. If "other" occurs frequently, make a note. There might be one or two categories that recur often and deserve to be added to the sheet as a specific category.

Checklist for Check Sheets

Clearly define the events to be recorded on the check sheet to avoid inappropriate registration.

❑ Determine the data collection period.

❑ If the collection period is lengthy, divide it into suitable intervals.

❑ Draw up the check sheet to allow ample space for recording each category.

❑ Collect data during the entire collection period, emphasizing accurate registration.

❑ Total the occurrences in each collection interval for each category and for the entire period.

❑ Identify the most frequently occurring categories.

❑ Note anomalies, for example, events not occurring at all, very infrequently, or in patterns.

Problem solving

Root cause analysis

Problem understanding

Possible cause generation and consensus reaching

Problem and cause data collection

Possible cause analysis

Cause-and-effect analysis

Tool selection

Case Business Quality Travel

Check Sheet Template

Problem	Period 1	Period 2	Period 3	Total number of occurrences per problem
Total number of problems per period				

Problem and Cause Data Collection Checklist

Root cause analysis is not one clear process from start to finish, yet some distinctive stages in the analysis are discernible. This checklist should help you assess whether the most important elements of the problem and cause data collection stage have been accomplished before moving on.

❑ Use a problem and its possible causes, based on the outcome of the possible cause generation and consensus reaching, as the starting point of the problem and cause data collection stage.

❑ Assess the situation for which data will be collected and determine which tool to use.

❑ When selecting a tool, consider the amount of data needed, the nature of the population, the costs involved, and so on.

❑ Choose among the following approaches: check sheet, sampling, and surveys.

❑ Collect data using the chosen approach, emphasizing accuracy and validity of the data.

❑ The collected data forms the basis for further investigation in the problem understanding stage.

Problem solving

Root cause analysis

Problem understanding

Possible cause generation and consensus reaching

Problem and cause data collection

Possible cause analysis

Cause-and-effect analysis

Tool selection

Case Business Quality Travel

Tools for Possible Cause Analysis

In chapter 6, we present five approaches for analyzing how different possible causes can impact the original problem.

Problem
solving

Root cause
analysis

Problem
understanding

Possible cause
generation
and consensus
reaching

Problem and
cause
data collection

Possible cause
analysis

Cause-and-
effect
analysis

Tool selection

Case Business
Quality Travel

Possible Cause Analysis

How are the possible causes connected to the problem and which causes seem to do the most harm? The purpose of the possible cause analysis phase, the last preparatory stage before attempting to solve the problem, is to clarify possible causes.

The tools available for possible cause analysis include:

- Histogram

- Pareto chart

- Scatter chart

- Relations diagram

- Affinity diagram

IT IS TEMPTING TO CHARGE AHEAD

At this point of the root cause analysis, you have completed much preparatory work. Having already generated a list of suspects, it is often tempting to charge ahead and try to solve the problem in one fell swoop by attacking all its possible causes. If you have already reached this point, be patient.

If you chase after all possible causes, you will probably spend too much energy, time, and money eliminating symptoms and lower level causes—perhaps even the root cause itself. Still, you'll be better off doing more analysis to precisely target the root cause before starting the elimination process.

So be patient, go the last mile, and find the root cause!

The Purpose and Applications of Histograms

A histogram, also called bar chart, is used to display the distribution and variation of a data set. The data can be measures of length, diameter, duration, costs, attitudes, and so on.

The main purpose of the histogram is to clarify the presentation of data. You can present the same information in a table; however, the graphic presentation format usually makes it easier to see relationships.

Typical applications of histograms in root cause analysis include:

- Presenting data to determine which causes dominate

- Understanding the distribution of occurrences of different problems, causes, consequences, and so on

---

THE NORMAL DISTRIBUTION OF DATA POINTS

In the treatment of histograms, it is important to mention a basic statistical concept—namely, normal distribution.

If you were to measure the time it takes to get to work each morning, you would probably focus on one value: the most likely duration of the trip. When a set of observations is distributed evenly around such a center point, or *expected value*, statisticians use normal distribution to describe these observations and calculate various likelihoods. If data from a normal distribution is presented in a histogram, the chart will taper off to both sides from this center value. Deviations from this pattern signal an anomaly, which can be used in the problem solving process, as explained later.

The normal distribution is a somewhat special distribution for various reasons.

It is symmetric; that is, the likelihood of a data point being larger than the expected value is as high as for a result being smaller than the expected value.

The histogram based on such a distribution looks like a bell, thus another term for this distribution is *bell-shaped*.

This distribution can be used to make powerful calculations; this process improvement method is called *statistical process control*.

Problem solving

Root cause analysis

Problem understanding

Possible cause generation and consensus reaching

Problem and cause data collection

Possible cause analysis

Cause-and-effect analysis

Tool selection

Case Business Quality Travel

The Steps in Using Histograms

1. Count the number of data points, N. (To produce a valid histogram, you should have at least 30 data points.)

2. Calculate the numerical distance, R, between the largest and smallest values in the data.

3. Depending on the value of N, divide R into a number of equally large classes, C, which can be found from this table:

The number of data points, N	The number of classes, C
Less than 50	5–7
50–100	6–10
100–250	7–12
More than 250	10–20

4. Calculate the width of each class, H, by using this formula:

$$H = \frac{R}{C}$$

The width should always have as many decimals as the data points.

5. Determine the lower and upper values for the individual classes by setting the smallest value of the data set as the lower value for the first class. Find the upper value for this class by adding the class width to the lower value. The higher value of one class in turn becomes the lower value of the next class. Remember that the lower value is always included in its class (that is, ≥ lower value), while the upper value belongs to the next class (that is, < upper value).

6. To simplify the construction of the histogram, insert the data into a check sheet.

7. Construct the histogram based on the check sheet. Mark the classes along the horizontal axis and the frequency along the vertical. Use vertical bars to indicate the distribution among classes.

Interpreting a Histogram

Histogram patterns to be aware of include:

- One peak shows the mean value for the process. If this peak is not centered, there must be a cause for it, which could prove interesting to look into.

- Two clear peaks could stem from two different data sources, which generally indicate an error during the data collection. This should be checked.

- A cut-off pattern that shows no signs of tapering off suggests that data points are being subjected to some selection during or after collection.

- A comb-like pattern indicates that too many classes have been defined. Some classes are unable to capture data points, rendering the chart useless.

AN EXAMPLE OF THE USE OF A HISTOGRAM

A small-town newspaper used children and adolescents to deliver the paper to subscribers. Frequent complaints about late deliveries suddenly started to occur from the area of one particular paper route. When the carrier was confronted with the complaints, he was surprised, had no good explanation for the delays, but promised to keep up the standards. After a brief period of significantly reduced complaints, they picked up again to the old level. The distribution manager asked a sample of subscribers on the route to make a note of every time the paper was delayed, and by how much. After four weeks of registration, the distribution manager analyzed the data. (The resulting histogram is shown below.) When confronting the paperboy with this, he confessed that on Mondays, Fridays, and Sundays, his sister did the route for him. Being less familiar with the route and cycling slower, this caused delays on the average of 20 minutes.

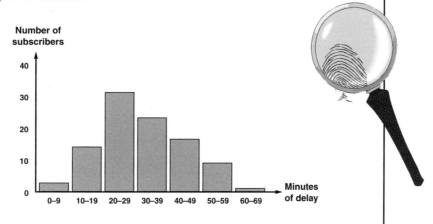

Problem
solving

Root cause
analysis

Problem
understanding

Possible cause
generation
and consensus
reaching

Problem and
cause
data collection

Possible cause
analysis

Cause-and-
effect
analysis

Tool selection

Case Business
Quality Travel

Checklist for Histograms

❏ Collect and record the data for which the histogram will be produced.

❏ There should be at least thirty data points in the data set, thus making it valid for use with a histogram.

❏ Calculate the numerical distance between the largest and smallest values in the data set.

❏ Use the help table to determine the number of classes in the histogram.

❏ Calculate the width of each class using the given formula.

❏ Determine the lower and upper values of each class, defining the border between them.

❏ Construct the histogram based on the defined classes and the collected data.

❏ Examine the resulting histogram to find any patterns. Analyze those patterns in terms of their causes.

Histogram Template

Classes

Frequency

Problem solving

Root cause analysis

Problem understanding

Possible cause generation and consensus reaching

Problem and cause data collection

Possible cause analysis

Cause-and-effect analysis

Tool selection

Case Business Quality Travel

Problem
solving

Root cause
analysis

Problem
understanding

Possible cause
generation
and consensus
reaching

Problem and
cause
data collection

Possible cause
analysis

Cause-and-
effect
analysis

Tool selection

Case Business
Quality Travel

The Purpose and Applications of Pareto Charts

The Pareto principle states that most effects, often 80 percent, are the result of a small number of causes, often only 20 percent. A healthy approach to root cause analysis is therefore to attack these 20 percent, often labeled "the vital few."

The main purpose of the Pareto chart is to graphically display this skewed distribution. The chart shows the causes to a problem sorted by the degree of seriousness, expressed as frequency of occurrence, costs, performance level, and so on.

In root cause analysis, the Pareto chart can be used to

- Obtain a clearer picture of the set of causes by viewing them according to importance.

- Understand which causes need further investigation.

VILFREDO PARETO—AN UNKNOWN QUALITY FRONT-RUNNER

If you are schooled in quality management, you have most certainly been told many great stories about famous quality gurus like Deming, Feigenbaum, Juran, and so on. However, the man who formulated the Pareto principle was probably the first scientist to influence the quality movement.

Vilfredo Pareto, an Italian mathematician, formulated his Pareto principle during the 1800s. He was concerned with the distribution of the riches in society, and claimed that 20 percent of the population owned 80 percent of the wealth.

Translated to modern quality terminology, the Pareto principle states that most effects are caused by a small number of causes. For example, usually 80 percent of the problems related to purchased materials are caused by 20 percent of the suppliers. More importantly, 80 percent of the costs connected to poor quality or generally low performance are caused by 20 percent of all possible causes.

When embarking on a problem-solving effort, start by attacking these 20 percent, which are often labeled "the vital few." This does not imply that the remaining 80 percent, the "important many," should be ignored. The Pareto principle simply suggests the order in which problems should be attacked.

The Steps in Using Pareto Charts

1. Define the problem to be analyzed and the different potential causes that have been identified.

2. Decide which criterion to use when comparing the possible causes, normally issues such as how often the different causes occur, their consequences, or costs.

3. Define the time interval during which data will be collected and carry out the data collection for the selected criterion. Often, this task will already have been performed.

4. Place the causes from left to right on the horizontal axis of the chart, in descending relative importance. Draw rectangles to heights that represent this importance.

5. Mark the data value on the left vertical axis and the percentage value on the right, and draw a curve of cumulative importance along the top edge of the rectangles.

AN EXAMPLE OF THE USE OF A PARETO CHART

Many studios around the world make television commercials. One studio specialized in shooting ads starring cats. This proved very popular and the company prospered.

Lately, many of the shootings were taking much longer than planned, causing production delays despite the use of overtime and weekend shootings. These delays were related to a few different factors including, among others, lack of equipment, technical problems with audio and video, rework of the script, and misbehaving cats.

In fact, this last issue seemed to be the most dominant problem area, and it was decided to map over the next few weeks what seemed to cause the unrest. The set assistant on duty was to record what he or she believed to be the reason the cats caused problems. This was done dutifully, and after five weeks, during which the problem persisted, quite a few pages of notes had been filled. Some of the data is shown on the top of the next page.

Not knowing exactly how to attack this data, someone recommended using a Pareto chart to see what seemed to be the prevailing causes. The chart is shown on the bottom of the next page, and led to changes related to the scheduling of shootings and the preparation of the cats.

Example Cat Studio Pareto Chart

Cause of cat distress	Time lost due to the cause (minutes)	Total time lost due to the cause (minutes)
Not been fed	4, 3, 5, 2, 5, 3	22
Not been cuddled	3, 3, 5, 3	14
Studio too cold	9, 2, 4, 6, 4, 5	30
Too much noise	20, 15, 35, 20, 9, 16	115
Smell of previous cat still present	41, 68, 39, 60, 29, 52, 19, 8	316
Surface to sit/lie on not appealing	2, 4, 1	7

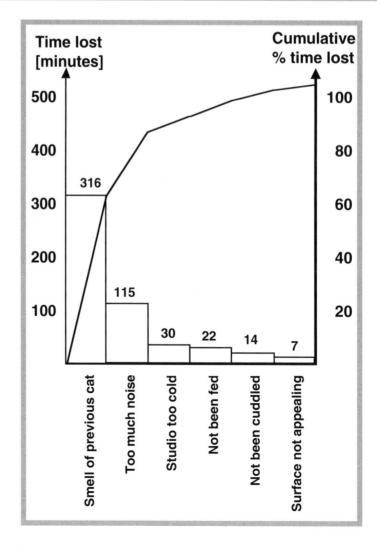

Checklist for Pareto Charts

Since use of the Pareto chart depends on a fixed set of causes, the problem and its probable causes must be defined.

❑ Agree which criterion will be used when ranking the possible causes.

❑ Set a time interval for collecting data about the causes and the defined criterion.

❑ Collect the data necessary to construct the chart, if you have not done so already.

❑ Draw the chart structure, placing the causes along the horizontal axis, the ranking criterion on the left vertical axis, and the cumulative criterion percentage on the right vertical axis.

❑ Place the causes in the chart from left to right in descending order of importance according to the defined criterion.

❑ Draw rectangles on the chart. Heights should correspond with the importance of each cause.

❑ Insert the individual data values for each cause rectangle into the chart on top of the rectangles.

❑ Draw a line marking the cumulative importance along the top edge of the rectangles.

Problem solving

Root cause analysis

Problem understanding

Possible cause generation and consensus reaching

Problem and cause data collection

Possible cause analysis

Cause-and-effect analysis

Tool selection

Case Business Quality Travel

Problem solving

Root cause analysis

Problem understanding

Possible cause generation and consensus reaching

Problem and cause data collection

Possible cause analysis

Cause-and-effect analysis

Tool selection

Case Business Quality Travel

Pareto Chart Template

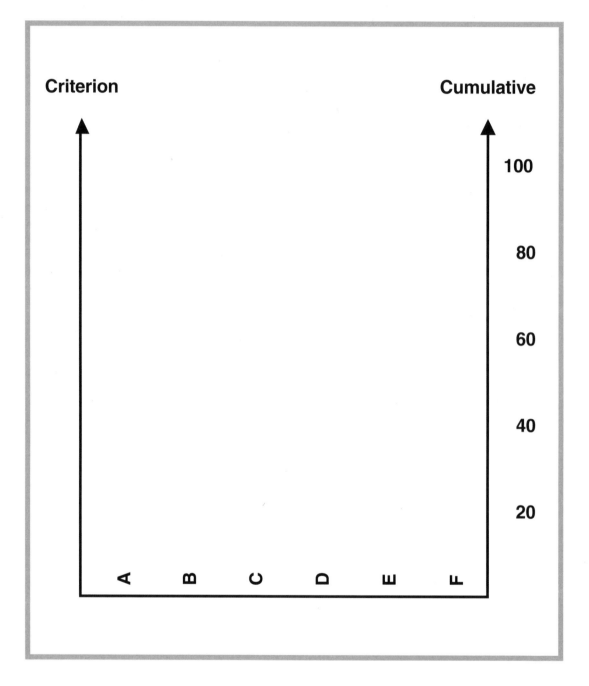

The Purpose and Applications of Scatter Charts

Causes at different levels impact one another frequently. A scatter chart can identify such links between causes. (A prerequisite is that each cause can be expressed by a numerical value.)

The main purpose of the scatter chart is to show the relationship between two causes or other variables.

In root cause analysis, scatter charts are useful to

- Explore the chain of causes by understanding the impact one cause at one level has on the cause(s) at the next level.

- Rule out causes at different levels that are not linked to the root cause.

Problem solving

Root cause analysis

Problem understanding

Possible cause generation and consensus reaching

Problem and cause data collection

Possible cause analysis

Cause-and-effect analysis

Tool selection

Case Business Quality Travel

TYPES OF COVARIANCE

A two-dimensional scatter chart can analyze only two causes, expressed by a suitable variable, at the same time. When one of the variables increases, the other can also increase, decrease, or display random variation. If the two variables seem to change in synchronization, it might indicate that they are related to and impact each other.

The correlation between the variables being examined can range from highly positive to highly negative. Between these two extremes, there are weaker degrees of both positive and negative correlation, as well as no correlation. Examples of different scatter charts for different degrees of correlation are shown here.

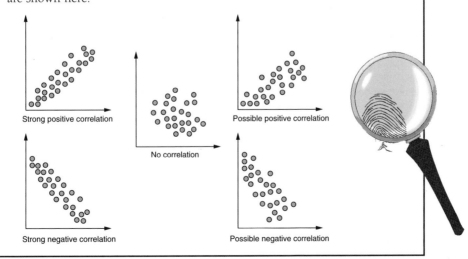

Strong positive correlation

No correlation

Possible positive correlation

Strong negative correlation

Possible negative correlation

The Steps in Using Scatter Charts

1. Select the two variables (one independent and one dependent) to be examined.

2. For each value of the independent variable, measure the corresponding value of the dependent value.

3. These two values form a data pair to be plotted in the chart. Typically, there should be at least 30, but preferably more than 100, data pairs to produce a meaningful chart.

4. Draw the chart by placing the independent, or expected cause, variable on the horizontal axis, and the dependent, or expected effect, variable on the vertical axis.

5. Plot and analyze the collected data pairs on the chart.

6. If the chart shows no correlation, draw the data pairs in a logarithmic chart, which can sometimes reveal connections not visible in a chart with ordinary axes.

AN EXAMPLE OF THE USE OF A SCATTER CHART

A large aluminum works company ran five shifts all year long, with the shifts divided into teams manning one furnace each. About a year ago, a new pay system was introduced whereby the teams were continuously measured on their output, energy use, defect rate, and scrap metal use. The pay for the entire team in turn was linked to the performance along these dimensions.

The pay system was well liked, but now and then there had been complaints that when shifts started, the previous shift filled up the furnace with scrap metal. This made the first shift look good in terms of scrap metal use, but lowered the output levels for the following team. There were also complaints about poor cleaning, required maintenance not performed, vehicles parked haphazardly, and so on.

Although all of these issues were raised by management, the problems irregularly persisted. Believing that the pay system, although having raised productivity by close to 2 percent, was the cause of the trouble, the system was terminated in the early spring. After a few weeks of operations under the old system, there seemed to be more complaints than ever about sloppiness when leaving a shift. Baffled, the management ran a series of tests to try to pinpoint the reasons for this. They designed a number of scatter charts that link the number of complaints with various causes. One of the last charts revealed the culprit: As the scatter chart on the following page shows, there seemed to be a clear correlation between the number of complaints and the weather, obviously because the shift teams wanted to get off and into the good weather as soon as possible, thus not cleaning up properly after themselves.

Example Aluminum Works Scatter Chart

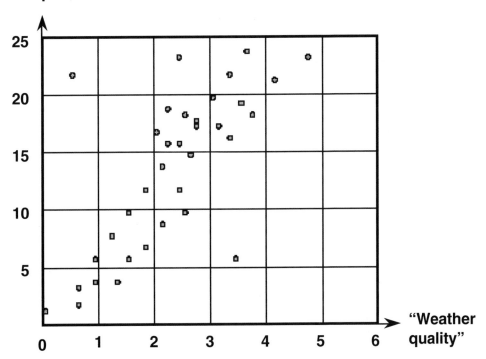

Complaints

"Weather quality"

Problem
solving

Root cause
analysis

Problem
understanding

Possible cause
generation
and consensus
reaching

Problem and
cause
data collection

Possible cause
analysis

Cause-and-
effect
analysis

Tool selection

Case Business
Quality Travel

A WORD OF WARNING ON CORRELATION

Two variables changing in a pattern of covariance might be correlated, which is an important finding. However, please keep in mind that even if there is some degree of synchronized variation between variables, it does not mean for certain that there is a cause-and-effect relationship between them. Indeed, a *third* variable may be causing the effects.

An astonishing example of an obvious correlation was a scatter chart that showed a perfect pattern between the Dow Jones total index and the water level of Lake Superior from 1925 to 1965.

Thus, if a scatter chart shows signs of correlation, investigate further for confirmation. Correspondingly, a chart that indicates no correlation should not lead you to dismiss your suspicions.

Problem
solving

Root cause
analysis

Problem
understanding

Possible cause
generation
and consensus
reaching

Problem and
cause
data collection

Possible cause
analysis

Cause-and-
effect
analysis

Tool selection

Case Business
Quality Travel

Checklist for Scatter Charts

If there is a larger experiment involving a number of correlation tests, the entire set of variables must be defined.

❏ Select and define the two variables to be analyzed in the individual chart.

❏ Measure the two variables, if data has not already been collected.

❏ The set of data pairs must consist of at least 30, but preferably more than 100 pairs.

❏ Design the chart by placing the independent variable on the horizontal axis. The independent variable is the factor believed to be governing the relationship between the two variables.

❏ On the vertical axis, insert the dependent variable—that is, the factor believed to change in proportion to the independent variable.

❏ Plot the data pairs themselves in the chart area.

❏ Examine the completed chart, looking for patterns that indicate a connection between the two variables.

❏ If no such patterns emerge, draw the chart over again using logarithmic scales on the two axes.

❏ If correlation patterns are identified, investigate any third variable involvement before drawing definite conclusions.

Scatter Chart Template

**Dependent
variable**

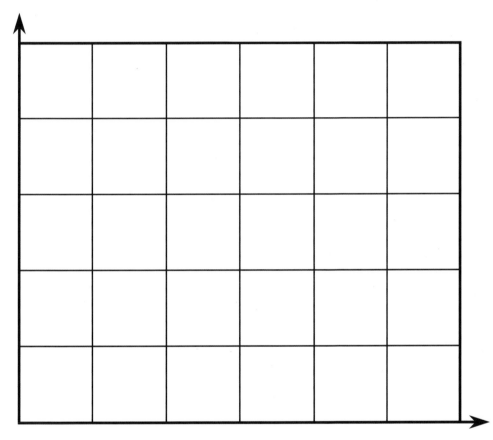

**Independent
variable**

Problem
solving

Root cause
analysis

Problem
understanding

Possible cause
generation
and consensus
reaching

Problem and
cause
data collection

Possible cause
analysis

Cause-and-
effect
analysis

Tool selection

Case Business
Quality Travel

Problem
solving

Root cause
analysis

Problem
understanding

Possible cause
generation
and consensus
reaching

Problem and
cause
data collection

Possible cause
analysis

Cause-and-
effect
analysis

Tool selection

Case Business
Quality Travel

The Purpose and Applications of Relations Diagrams

A relations diagram borders on being a tool for cause-and-effect analysis, but is mainly used to identify logical relationships in a complex and confusing problem situation. In such cases, the strength of a relations diagram is its ability to visualize such relationships.

A relations diagram's main purpose is to help identify relationships that are not easily recognizable.

In root cause analysis, this is particularly useful to

• Understand how different aspects of the problem are connected.

• See relationships between the problem and its possible causes that can be further analyzed.

TWO TYPES OF RELATIONS DIAGRAMS

There are two types of relations diagrams:

• Qualitative relations diagrams

• Quantitative relations diagrams

Both diagrams are based on the principle of identifying relationships among different factors, but they differ in their approach. In the qualitative version, the factors to be analyzed are simply placed in an empty chart area and relationships are found by connecting the factors based on an intuitive understanding of them. As such, this variant can produce unreliable results.

In the quantitative type, a simpler numerical approach is used to determine the relationships between different factors. Since this approach is more structured, it is usually easier to drive this process toward a completed analysis. For these reasons, the quantitative relations diagram is the one presented in this book.

The Steps in Using Relations Diagrams

1. Determine the factors to be analyzed for possible relationships and label these using brief and succinct definitions.

2. Place the factors in an empty chart area on a whiteboard, preferably in a coarse circular shape.

3. Assess what each factor impacts (or which factors are impacted by it) and illustrate the relationships using arrows.

4. After all relationships have been assessed, count the number of arrows pointing into and away from each factor and denote this information in the diagram.

5. Depending on the number of arrows pointing in each direction for a factor, it can play one of two roles: **driver** (more arrows away from than into), or **indicator** (more arrows into than away from).

6. When continuing the root cause analysis, the drivers form the starting point.

AN EXAMPLE OF THE USE OF A RELATIONS DIAGRAM

A small hospital was concerned with the productivity of its doctors, as they were the most expensive employees and were critical for the treatment of the patients. Having taken numerous steps toward ensuring high productivity, hospital management was baffled month after month when productivity steadily declined.

Since this astonishing development was unexplainable, management decided to gain some insight into causes and effects among the different factors at play. A relations diagram was seen as an ideal vehicle for this, and the following factors were included in the analysis:

• The number of scheduled appointments per doctor

• The number of emergency appointments per doctor

• Administrative workload per doctor

• The number of changes in scheduled appointments

• Equipment quality and reliability

• Nurse availability

• Availability of other support functions

• The pay level of doctors

When the relations diagram seen on the following page had been completed, attention shifted from improving the doctor's work situation to ensuring the availability of nurses, other support functions, and operational equipment.

Example Hospital Relations Diagram

Problem
solving

Root cause
analysis

Problem
understanding

Possible cause
generation
and consensus
reaching

Problem and
cause
data collection

Possible cause
analysis

Cause-and-
effect
analysis

Tool selection

Case Business
Quality Travel

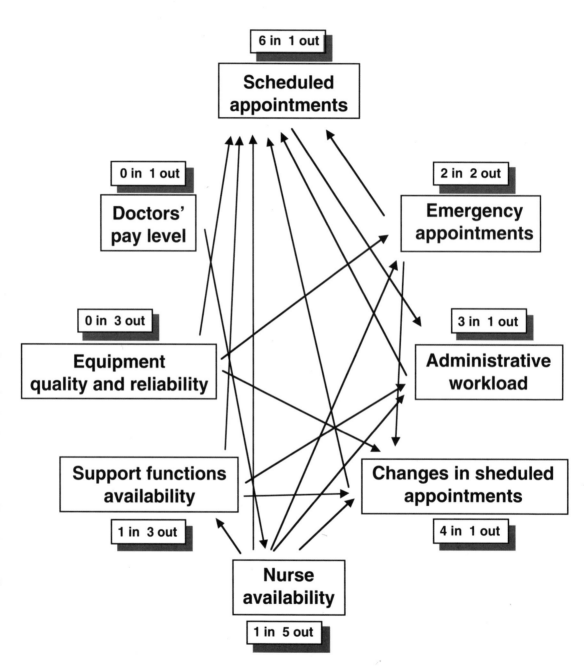

Checklist for Relations Diagrams

❑ Determine the factors you want included in the analysis for possible relationships.

❑ Label these factors using brief and succinct definitions.

❑ Place the factors, identified by their labels, in small boxes throughout an empty chart area on a whiteboard, preferably in a coarse circular shape.

❑ For each factor in the analysis, assess what factors it impacts and are impacted by it.

❑ Illustrate the impacts using arrows between the factors, pointing from the impacting factor to the one being impacted.

❑ Count the number of arrows pointing toward and away from each factor and write this information in the chart next to the factor.

❑ Divide the factors into **drivers** and **indicators** based on whether more impact arrows point away or toward them.

❑ Later in the analysis, use the drivers as a starting point for identifying the causes to the problem.

Problem solving

Root cause analysis

Problem understanding

Possible cause generation and consensus reaching

Problem and cause data collection

Possible cause analysis

Cause-and-effect analysis

Tool selection

Case Business Quality Travel

Relations Diagram Template

Problem solving

Root cause analysis

Problem understanding

Possible cause generation and consensus reaching

Problem and cause data collection

Possible cause analysis

Cause-and-effect analysis

Tool selection

Case Business Quality Travel

in out

in out

in out

in out

in out

in out

The Purpose and Applications of Affinity Diagrams

The previously presented possible cause analysis tools are mostly applicable when the data is in a numerical form. To analyze more qualitative data, an affinity diagram is useful. It groups data and finds underlying relationships connecting the resulting groups.

This tool allows the user to see relationships among seemingly unrelated ideas, conditions, or meanings.

In root cause analysis, some uses of affinity diagrams include:

• Exploring relationships among different causes, often at different levels in the cause hierarchy

• Grouping related causes into classes that might be treated collectively later on in the analysis

Problem solving

Root cause analysis

Problem understanding

Possible cause generation and consensus reaching

Problem and cause data collection

Possible cause analysis

Cause-and-effect analysis

Tool selection

Case Business Quality Travel

THE ORIGINS OF THE AFFINITY DIAGRAM

While most of the root cause analysis tools stem from precise scientific fields like mathematics, statistics, and so on, the affinity diagram was invented in a field far from these.

The tool is known by several names. In addition to affinity diagram or chart, it is also called a KJ chart, so named for Jiro Kawakita, a Japanese anthropologist who invented the KJ method, a precursor to the KJ chart.

This also has some implications on the use of the tool. While many tools require a precise mind geared toward accuracy, the affinity diagram is typically a creative technique that requires an open mind on the part of participants.

Problem
solving

Root cause
analysis

Problem
understanding

Possible cause
generation
and consensus
reaching

Problem and
cause
data collection

Possible cause
analysis

Cause-and-
effect
analysis

Tool selection

Case Business
Quality Travel

The Steps in Using Affinity Diagrams

1. Gather the participants in a room that has a large whiteboard. Write the topic to be analyzed in large letters at the top of the board, preferably in neutral terms, and underlined.

2. Take possible causes from the previous stage, or brainstorm them, and write these causes on adhesive notes. These should be succinctly formulated, but never only as one single word. Attach the notes to the board in a totally random pattern.

3. In silence, without any discussion, the group moves the notes around trying to form groups of causes that are related. Usually the notes are moved many times before they find their places. Depending on the number of ideas, this might easily take an hour or more.

4. After grouping ideas, the participants discuss the final shape of the chart. As the motives for placing notes in specific spots are explained, minor adjustments should be allowed. The total number of groups should not exceed five to ten.

5. Make titles for the groups, dividing larger groups into subgroups at lower levels.

6. Make the chart by drawing boxes around the groups and possibly adding arrows between them to indicate further relationships.

7. Evaluate the chart with regard to further effort. The groups contain elements and suggestions to causes that affect one another, and thus must be seen in connection when devising solutions.

Example Furniture Manufacturer Affinity Diagram

(see the following example)

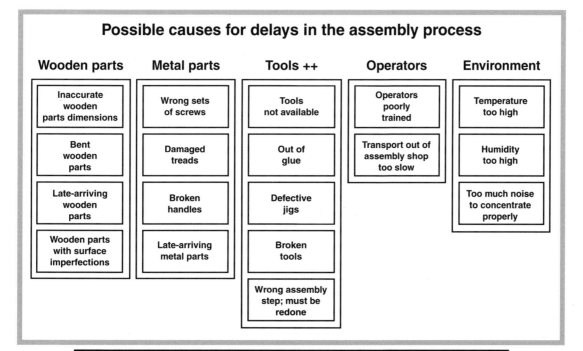

Possible causes for delays in the assembly process

Wooden parts	Metal parts	Tools ++	Operators	Environment
Inaccurate wooden parts dimensions	Wrong sets of screws	Tools not available	Operators poorly trained	Temperature too high
Bent wooden parts	Damaged treads	Out of glue	Transport out of assembly shop too slow	Humidity too high
Late-arriving wooden parts	Broken handles	Defective jigs		Too much noise to concentrate properly
Wooden parts with surface imperfections	Late-arriving metal parts	Broken tools		
		Wrong assembly step; must be redone		

AN EXAMPLE OF THE USE OF AN AFFINITY DIAGRAM

A furniture manufacturer delivered, among many other product lines, a series of chests of drawers. The assembly of these generally took much longer than the calculated assembly time, on which all production plans and delivery schedules were based. From a brief evaluation of the situation, it was clear that there were many different reasons why the assembly process took so long.

Some of the assembly workers and employees from departments supplying parts and services to them teamed up to look into these causes in more detail. They realized that many of the identified reasons were related—some directly, others more loosely. To better understand these relationships, empoloyees made an affinity diagram to help clarify the situation.

The resulting diagram, shown above, emerged from a run-through of the main steps in the process for designing such a chart. The groups of probable causes represented a good starting point for determining which groups caused the most harm.

Problem
solving

Root cause
analysis

Problem
understanding

Possible cause
generation
and consensus
reaching

Problem and
cause
data collection

Possible cause
analysis

Cause-and-
effect
analysis

Tool selection

Case Business
Quality Travel

Checklist for Affinity Diagrams

A suitable room for the exercise must be provided, containing a large whiteboard and adhesive notes.

❑ Write the topic—that is, a problem or its causes—on top of the whiteboard.

❑ Either analyze causes to the problem that were gathered in the possible cause generation stage, or brainstorm them now.

❑ Write the possible causes on the adhesive notes, in neutral terms, and attach them to the whiteboard in a random pattern.

❑ Run a session where the participants silently move the causes around to group them.

❑ Discuss the grouping and possible adjustments allowed, arriving at no more than five to ten groups of causes.

❑ Make titles for each of the groups.

❑ Draw boxes around the groups and add arrows to symbolize additional relationships to complete the chart.

❑ Decide on a further course of action concerning the groups of possible causes and their treatment.

Possible Cause Analysis Checklist

Although root cause analysis is not one clear process from start to finish, some distinctive stages in the analysis are discernible. This checklist should help assess whether the most important elements of the possible cause analysis stage have been accomplished before moving on.

❑ Use one or more data sets pertaining to the problem at hand and its possible causes as the starting point of the possible cause analysis stage.

❑ Assess the collected data and desired analysis to determine which tool to use. Consider whether one-dimensional effects are likely to be found, if correlation among two or more groups of data are expected, the complexity of the data, and so on.

❑ Choose among the following analysis tools: histograms, Pareto charts, scatter charts, relations diagrams, and affinity diagrams.

❑ Conduct the analysis according to the steps of the selected tool or tools.

❑ If more than one tool is applied, compare the conclusions from each analysis for opposing or matching results.

❑ Bring the conclusions from the possible cause analysis stage forward into the cause-and-effect analysis stage.

Problem solving

Root cause analysis

Problem understanding

Possible cause generation and consensus reaching

Problem and cause data collection

Possible cause analysis

Cause-and-effect analysis

Tool selection

Case Business Quality Travel

Tools for Cause-and-Effect Analysis

This chapter presents three individual tools and techniques for the last stage of the root cause analysis: the cause-and-effect analysis. Other tools are available as well, but they are considerably more complex and often require advanced calculations. Such tools have been eliminated from our discussion here so we can keep these approaches simple and straightforward to apply.

Cause-and-Effect Analysis

You are finally here! From the list of possible causes you have created and analyzed during the four previous stages, you are now ready to conclude the analysis and begin to eliminate the root cause.

In terms of duration and complexity, this stage is rarely the most difficult one or longest-lasting task to complete. Thanks to thorough preparation, you can normally proceed through this stage quickly.

The tools available for the analysis are

- Cause-and-effect chart

- Matrix diagram

- Five whys

YOU REAP WHAT YOU SOW

A company operating a large fleet of vending machines found that an increasing number of machines were vandalized. To look further into the situation, a small task force was assembled.

With little structured analysis beyond a quick brainstorming, the group decided that the problem was that many of the machines were located in areas with little traffic, poor lighting, and so on. Many machines were subsequently relocated, but the problem persisted.

A second team was assembled, and was instructed to make more qualified recommendations. After spending nearly four months applying many of the tools covered in this book, the team concluded that two situations caused sufficient frustration and anger to customers that they took it out on the vending machines:

- The machine rejected their money, specifically slightly crumpled bills.

- Items listed in the normal selection were sold out.

By redesigning the procedure for machine replenishment and maintenance, both situations occurred much less frequently, and vandalism decreased accordingly.

The Purpose and Applications of Cause-and-Effect Charts

The name of the cause-and-effect chart tool defines what it is about: a chart that analyzes relationships between a problem and its causes. It combines aspects of brainstorming with systematic analysis to create a powerful technique. The tool is also known as the Ishikawa diagram, named for its inventor.

In the larger framework of root cause analysis, this tool's main purpose is to understand what causes a problem. It can be used to

- Generate and group problem causes.

- Systematically evaluate the causes and determine which are most likely to be root causes.

TWO TYPES OF CAUSE-AND-EFFECT CHARTS

The cause-and-effect chart has so far been described as if it were one singular chart, but there are at least two types of cause-and-effect charts.

- *Fishbone chart:* the traditional way of constructing such charts, where the main product is a chart whose shape resembles a fishbone.

- *Process chart:* more directly aimed at the analysis of problems inside business processes. For each step of the process that is believed to create problems, a fishbone chart is constructed to address all potential causes of less-than-expected performance. After individual charts are designed, a collective analysis is conducted to identify the causes of highest importance.

The traditional fishbone chart type is discussed here, including two distinctly different ways of creating the chart.

- *Dispersion analysis:* where the problem being analyzed is drawn on the right-hand side of the chart, at the end of a large arrow. Main groups of probable causes are drawn as branches to the arrow. For each branch, all possible causes are identified.

- *Cause enumeration:* where all probable causes are brainstormed and listed in the order they are generated. The causes are then grouped into main categories and written on the fishbone chart.

The end product is the same regardless of the approach used. Our focus here is dispersion analysis.

Problem
solving

Root cause
analysis

Problem
understanding

Possible cause
generation
and consensus
reaching

Problem and
cause
data collection

Possible cause
analysis

Cause-and-
effect
analysis

Tool selection

Case Business
Quality Travel

The Steps in Using Cause-and-Effect Charts

1. Clearly describe the problem for which causes are sought.

2. Using a whiteboard or some other large medium, draw the problem at the right end of a large arrow. Allow space for the causes to be generated. Do not strive for symmetry and graphic effects.

3. Identify the main categories of causes to the problem and write them at branches emanating from the large arrow.

4. Brainstorm and write all possible causes in the applicable area(s) of the chart. Use brief and succinct descriptions. Proceed through the chart one main category at a time. Write causes that belong to more than one category in all relevant positions.

5. Analyze the identified causes to determine the most likely root causes.

AN EXAMPLE OF THE USE OF A CAUSE-AND-EFFECT CHART

A company operating cable television services had seen consistently high employee absenteeism, especially in the installation and service department. Besides costing the company a lot of money, this absenteeism angered many customers, because hook-ups were not done at the agreed time and problems took unacceptably long to correct.

Among other steps taken to improve the situation, the human resource manager and some service personnel turned to different problem solving tools. They first conducted a brainstorming session that generated many ideas as to why absenteeism was so high, then analyzed these ideas by using a cause-and-effect chart.

The brainstorming session generated many ideas, some more creative, and perhaps less realistic, than others. After sorting these and picking those most likely to be relevant and curable causes, the group analyzed and grouped the causes on the chart. The resulting diagram is shown on the following page. The results led the company to consider training programs, reward systems, and the quality of the tools and equipment used by the service personnel.

Example Cable Television Company Cause-and-Effect Chart

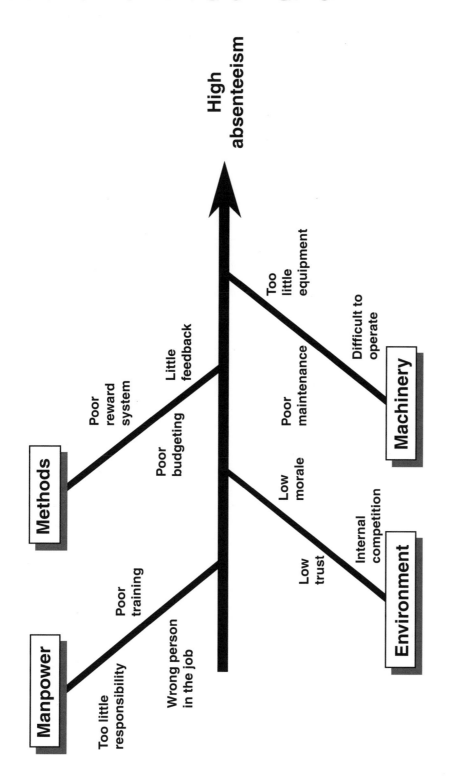

Problem
solving

Root cause
analysis

Problem
understanding

Possible cause
generation
and consensus
reaching

Problem and
cause
data collection

Possible cause
analysis

 Cause-and-
effect
analysis

Tool selection

Case Business
Quality Travel

Checklist for Cause-and-Effect Charts

❏ Clearly define and describe the problem under analysis to allow a targeted analysis session.

❏ Write the problem at the end of a large arrow on a whiteboard or some other suitable medium.

❏ When drawing the chart, allow sufficient space to write many ideas and causes; don't worry about making your chart neat at this stage of the analysis.

❏ Define main groups of causes and write them at the ends of "branches" pointing to the large arrow.

❏ Write possible causes to the problem along appropriate branches of the fishbone, based either on a previously conducted brainstorming session or on brainstorming done while constructing the chart.

❏ Strive for brief and succinct descriptions when writing the causes in the chart.

❏ After assigning all causes to the appropriate branch(es), evaluate the different groups of causes one at a time.

❏ Identify the most important causes and declare possible root causes.

Cause-and-Effect Chart Template

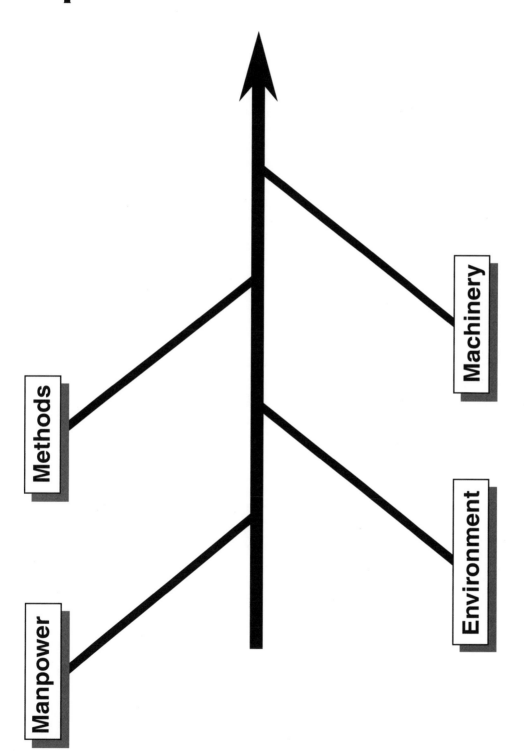

Methods

Manpower

Machinery

Environment

Problem
solving

Root cause
analysis

Problem
understanding

Possible cause
generation
and consensus
reaching

Problem and
cause
data collection

Possible cause
analysis

Cause-and-
effect
analysis

Tool selection

Case Business
Quality Travel

The Purpose and Applications of Matrix Diagrams

The second tool at this stage of the analysis allows you to investigate a number of possible causes and determine which contributes most to the problem being analyzed. The tool's strength lies in its ability to graphically portray multiple connections.

The main purpose of the matrix diagram is to analyze causal relationships between possible causes and problems.

In root cause analysis, this can be used for

- Mapping the overall impact of different possible causes of the problem.

- Determining which of many causes is the most prominent, thus usually the root cause.

SEVERAL TYPES OF MATRIX DIAGRAMS

Many different matrix diagrams can be used, depending on the number of variables. Some common ones are shown here.

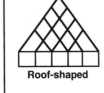

Roof-shaped

L-shaped

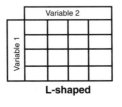

Y-shaped

T-shaped   **X-shaped**

In root cause analysis, the most widely used type of diagram is the L-shaped matrix, which places the problem characteristics on one side and the possible causes on the other. Other types of matrix diagrams are not described here.

The Steps in Using Matrix Diagrams

1. Select the problem characteristics and possible causes to be analyzed for types and levels of relationships.

2. Draw an empty matrix of suitable size.

3. Insert the variables into the diagram.

4. Indicate impacts by using the symbols shown below.

5. For each column in the diagram, calculate the total impact and present the sum.

6. Possible causes with a large sum are likely root causes.

Relation	Symbol	Weight
Weak	△	1
Medium	○	3
Strong	◉	9

AN EXAMPLE OF THE USE OF A MATRIX DIAGRAM

A taxi operator in a large city had seen that competing for customers on streets, at airports, and so on, generated long periods of waiting time during which potential revenue was lost. It had therefore specialized in pre-order customers like hotels, hospitals, and private companies. This strategy had been successful, but lately the company had received many customer complaints related to tardy pick-up and delivery, poorly cleaned cars, discourteous drivers, and other less serious issues. Reliability, service, and their customers' ability to trust them were crucial for success, so this problem had to be solved.

It seemed to the administration, the dispatching central, and the drivers that the main cause for the delays was unpredictable traffic. Many other options had been mentioned as well, so a small improvement team used a matrix diagram to see if any of these other possible causes were important.

The resulting matrix diagram is shown on the following page. As you can see, when the larger situation had been carefully considered, there were at least four other factors that probably caused many of the problems. Putting measures in place to remedy these factors did produce improvement.

Example Taxi Company Matrix Diagram

Problem solving

Root cause analysis

Problem understanding

Possible cause generation and consensus reaching

Problem and cause data collection

Possible cause analysis

➡ Cause-and-effect analysis

Tool selection

Case Business Quality Travel

Problem characteristic	Possible causes						
	Unpredictable traffic	Late dispatch	Too many rides per car	Poor route planning	No car wash machine	Inaccurate address information	Old cars
Late pick-up	●	●	○	●	△	●	○
Late delivery	●	●	○	●			○
Dirty car exterior			●	△	●		
Dirty car interior			●		●		○
Rude driver	△	○	○	△		●	
"Bumpy" ride				○			○
Baggage space							○
Total impact score	19	21	27	23	19	18	15

Checklist for Matrix Diagrams

The problem characteristics and the possible causes of the problem must be carefully selected, making sure not to exclude any possible causes from the analysis.

❏ Draw an empty matrix diagram, leaving space for the selected amount of problem characteristics and possible causes.

❏ Insert these variables into the matrix diagram.

❏ Assess each possible cause and its impact on each of the problem characteristics and place the appropriate impact symbol in the matrix.

❏ When all impact combinations have been evaluated, calculate the total impact scores for each possible cause by summing the corresponding impact factors for each of the impact symbols.

❏ Write the total impact scores in the matrix.

❏ Identify the possible causes with the largest total impact scores, as these are likely root causes of the problem.

Problem solving

Root cause analysis

Problem understanding

Possible cause generation and consensus reaching

Problem and cause data collection

Possible cause analysis

Cause-and-effect analysis

Tool selection

Case Business Quality Travel

Matrix Diagram Template

Possible causes

Problem characteristic

Total impact score

The Purpose and Applications of Five Whys

Problem solving

Root cause analysis

Problem understanding

Possible cause generation and consensus reaching

Problem and cause data collection

Possible cause analysis

Cause-and-effect analysis

Tool selection

Case Business Quality Travel

Five whys is also known as the why-why chart and root cause analysis. Its inherent nature is to dive ever more deeply into the levels of causes, thus resembling the wider concept of root cause analysis.

Its main purpose is to constantly ask **Why?** when a cause has been identified, thus progressing through the levels toward the root cause.

In a wider root cause analysis, five whys can be used to

- Question each identified cause as to whether it is a symptom, a lower-level cause, or a root cause.

- Continue the search for true root causes even after finding that a possible cause has been found.

STOP THE QUESTIONING IN TIME

The key concept of the five whys technique is to keep posing the question Why? whenever a new cause has been identified. For each time the why question is answered by bringing up another cause at a higher level in the cause hierarchy, immediately ask again, "Why?" This relentless approach keeps those working on the problem on their toes, thus not allowing them to settle for anything less than the root cause.

However, there comes a point in the chain of causes where no further causes can possibly be found. This last cause is, as you know, the root cause—the point at which you should stop asking why. For those who are religious, it is possible to argue that there is another level, namely God, behind everything that happens. In root cause analysis, it is wise to stop before you reach this level, as it could prove very difficult to do anything about.

Problem
solving

Root cause
analysis

Problem
understanding

Possible cause
generation
and consensus
reaching

Problem and
cause
data collection

Possible cause
analysis

Cause-and-
effect
analysis

Tool selection

Case Business
Quality Travel

The Steps in Using Five Whys

1. Determine the starting point of the analysis, either a problem or an already identified cause that should be further analyzed.

2. Use brainstorming, brainwriting, and other approaches to find causes at the level below the starting point.

3. Ask "Why is this a cause for the original problem?" for each identified cause.

4. Portray the chain of causes either in a simple chart or as a sequence of text on a whiteboard.

5. For each new answer to the question, ask the question again, continuing until no new answer results. This will most likely be the core of the root causes of the problem.

6. As a rule of thumb, this method often requires five rounds of the question "Why?".

AN EXAMPLE OF THE USE OF FIVE WHYS

As a small business in the rapidly growing business of web site design and programming, an enterprise of about 25 people had grown from a small home-based outfit into the current company with many large companies as clients. Previously, the team of web programmers had received much acclaim for its web page designs and innovative use of graphics to make sites easy to navigate. Lately, however, more and more clients were dissatisfied with the web sites. They complained about functionality, simple errors in layout or text, late completion of designs and entire sites, and so on.

The situation had gotten to a point where the employees faced more and more problems and no longer thought the work was as much fun as it used to be. Some of the most entrenched technological freaks blamed the problems on the company's unwillingness to stay abreast in this development; others thought most of the problems stemmed from the lack of qualified programmers.

To get to the bottom of this problem, which started to threaten the future of the company, one of the founding partners used the five whys tool. The resulting chart is shown on the following page. As you can see, the root causes were neither of those previously believed to be the culprits, but rather a too high number of projects being undertaken simultaneously and a poor system for time and project planning.

Example Web Design Company Five Whys

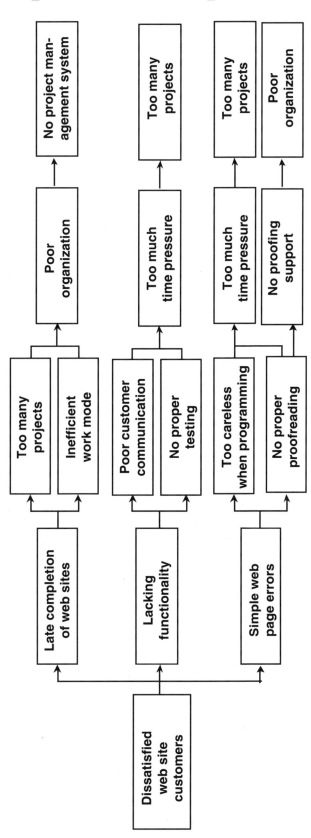

Checklist for Five Whys

Define a clear starting point for the analysis, either a problem or an identified cause at some level.

❏ Use brainstorming or other idea-generation approaches to find causes at the level below the starting point.

❏ For each identified cause, question why this is a cause to the original problem. This process, in turn, generates new causes.

❏ Either draw in a diagram or print as plain text the links of causes below one another.

❏ For each new answer to the why question, pose the question over again until no new answers result.

❏ This last cause (or causes) are the problem's root cause.

Five Whys Template

Why?

Why?

Why?

Why?

Why?

Problem
solving

Root cause
analysis

Problem
understanding

Possible cause
generation
and consensus
reaching

Problem and
cause
data collection

Possible cause
analysis

Cause-and-
effect
analysis

Tool selection

Case Business
Quality Travel

Cause-and-Effect Analysis Checklist

Although root cause analysis is not one clear process from start to finish, some distinctive stages are discernible. This checklist helps assess whether the most important elements of the cause-and-effect analysis stage have been accomplished before declaring the analysis complete.

❏ Use the results of the possible cause analysis stage to determine the starting point for the cause-and-effect analysis stage.

❏ Assess the identified possible causes to determine which tool to use. Consider the number of causes found, the degree of similarities among them, the extent to which some of them seem to stand out as obvious root causes, and so on.

❏ Choose among the following analysis tools: matrix diagrams, cause-and-effect charts, and five whys.

❏ Carry out the analysis according to the steps of the selected tool or tools.

❏ The conclusions from the cause-and-effect analysis stage should be true and relevant conclusions about the root cause of the problem being analyzed.

How to Select the Right Tool

Chapter 7 presented an abundance of different tools and techniques. It is difficult to know which tool should be used when, and how the tools relate to one another in an overall root cause analysis. This chapter gives advice and sets forth guidelines for selecting the appropriate tool in a given situation.

A Word of Caution about Tools

Before looking into tool selection, consider this warning on the topic of tools. The main objective of your exercise is to find the root cause of your problem and eliminate it. The tools we've presented are mere aids that can help you reach this goal. Don't let your focus on tools blur your sights on this target! Too much emphasis on the tools can lead to the problem becoming secondary.

Two key recommendations are

- Do not become a slave to one or more tools!

- Remember that a tool is not a solution in search of a problem to solve!

MASTER MANY TOOLS

While it is not necessary to know every tool presented in this book, we urge you to acquaint yourself with several of them, enabling you to be flexible in applying them. Each tool has its strengths and weaknesses. The tool should fit the problem, not the other way around.

The old saying, many roads lead to Rome, also applies in problem solving. There seldom is only one right way of applying problem-solving techniques. Indeed, we have a number of options in terms of procedure and choice of tools. To be flexible, you should be able to use a variety of tools in solving problems. All too often people become slaves to one tool. This wastes time and energy, and causes disillusionment. Like those who use their personal computers to draw, write, and play games, people often become more focused on the wrapping than what is in the package.

Introduction to Tool Selection

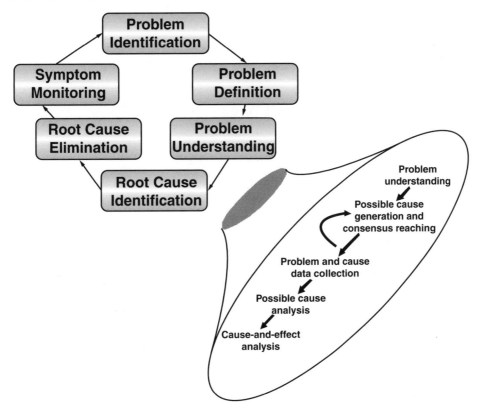

THE PROBLEM-SOLVING PROCESS VERSUS THE GROUPS OF TOOLS

The interrelationship between the problem-solving process and the groups of root cause analysis tools are shown in the figure above. As you can see, the tools described in this book mainly deal with problem understanding and root cause identification. When the root causes have been identified, they must be eliminated, and that involves a different process.

For each of the five groups of tools, this book provides guidelines for tool selection. By answering the questions in the ensuing flowcharts, you will be guided toward using suitable tools in a given situation. In some cases it might be appropriate to use several tools from a group, other times no tools will fit. The guidelines will help in this process, but we urge you to use your good sense as well.

Tool Selection in General

Problem
solving

Root cause
analysis

Problem
understanding

Possible cause
generation
and consensus
reaching

Problem and
cause
data collection

Possible cause
analysis

Cause-and-
effect
analysis

Tool selection

Case Business
Quality Travel

The guidelines for the selection of tools are based on a few parameters and should not be followed blindly. You, the reader, have considerable knowledge about the situation at hand, and might find another tool more suitable. If the group agrees, then this other tool should be used instead.

On the other hand, much of our advice on tool selection is helpful. One such suggestion is to keep focused on the problem and use the accumulated knowledge and experience of the group.

This book can serve as a tool in such a process.

TOOLS FOR GROUPS

The tools in this book should be used by groups of people. The use of some tools requires that all participants have prior knowledge of the tool at hand. For others, it is necessary that only the chairperson of the group know the tool. An example of the latter is the use of brainstorming. It might be sufficient for the chairperson of the group to inform the others about the purpose and rules of brainstorming. However, a group where all participants have prior knowledge of and experience with brainstorming will most likely be far more efficient. If you know the tool you are using, you will focus more on the problem than the tool.

Working in groups has many benefits, but to work properly, groups should have most of the following characteristics:

- An atmosphere of trust, openness, support, and honesty

- No fear of consequences when an individual shares something

- Participants who know one another

- Participants who take responsibility for the success of the team

- Participants who contribute in the discussions and listen actively

- Participants who give useful feedback and accept feedback easily

- Participants who get their messages across

Problem Understanding Tool Selection

As you remember, problem understanding is made up of approaches that help get to the bottom of the problem you want to solve. This stage focuses on understanding the nature of the problem, and is a preparatory step before starting the analysis. A flowchart for the problem understanding stage is shown below, and is explained on the following page.

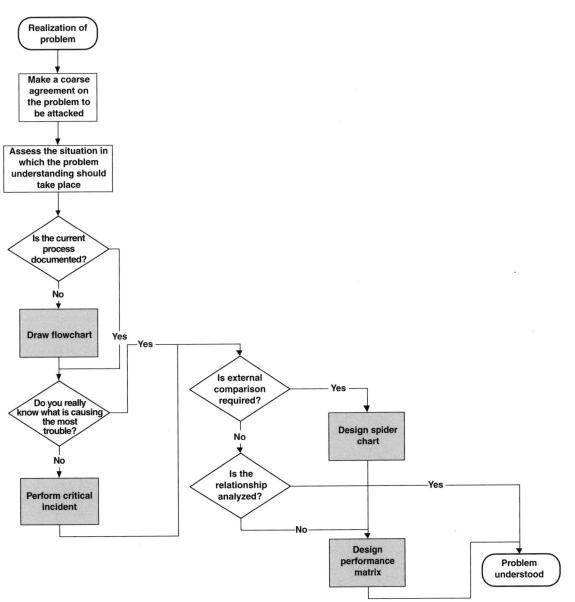

Problem
solving

Root cause
analysis

Problem
understanding

Possible cause
generation
and consensus
reaching

Problem and
cause
data collection

Possible cause
analysis

Cause-and-
effect
analysis

Tool selection

Case Business
Quality Travel

Tool Selection Flowchart for Problem Understanding Explained

First, agree on the problem to be attacked. Then, assess the situation in which the problem understanding will occur and select a suitable approach. Typical considerations are pre-analysis problem understanding and how many people have been involved in debates about the problem so far.

Second, ask whether the process is already documented. If not, draw one or more flowcharts to portray the flow of activities in the process containing the problem.

Third, ask whether you really know what is causing the most trouble. If not, perform critical incident. The main purpose of the critical incident method is to understand what is really causing the most trouble in a problematic situation.

Fourth, ask whether any form of external comparison is required. If so, design a spider chart. The main purpose is to give a graphic impression of how the performance of business processes or problem areas compares with other organizations.

Finally, ask whether the relationship between importance and performance level for the problem area or process should be analyzed. If not, the problem understanding stage is finished. If so, design a performance matrix to show the importance and current performance simultaneously to arrive at a sense of priority.

Possible Cause Generation and Consensus Reaching Tool Selection

Possible cause generation and consensus reaching is a collection of generic tools that can be applied at different stages in the analysis. Different ways of brainstorming can help you generate ideas about possible causes. The analysis is normally carried out in groups, so methods that help you arrive at consensus solutions are also useful. A flowchart for the possible cause generation and consensus reaching stage is shown below, and explained on the next page. Note that possible cause generation and consensus reaching is not a streamlined process. One might, for instance, choose to use brainstorming and NGT together as one tool, and one or more of the tools might be used at other stages in the process.

```
        ( Understand
            problem )
              │
              ▼
   ┌────────────────────┐
   │ Decide which problem│
   │ needs possible cause│
   │ generation and define│
   │ the objectives of    │
   │ the session          │
   └────────────────────┘
              │
              ▼
          ◇ Assess the
          situation to decide ───── Yes ──┐
          if brainwriting is             │
          required ◇                      │
              │                           │
              No                          │
              ▼                           ▼
      ┌──────────────┐          ┌──────────────┐
      │   Perform    │          │   Perform    │
      │ brainstorming│          │ brainwriting │
      └──────────────┘          └──────────────┘
              │                           │
              ▼                           │
          ◇ Is it necessary to ─── Yes ──┐│
          prioritize ideas? ◇            ││
              │                          ▼▼
              No               ◇ Assess
              │                analysis of ──── Yes ──┐
              │                idea set ◇             │
              │                     │                 │
              │                     No                ▼
              │                     ▼          ┌──────────────┐
              │            ┌──────────────┐    │  Perform NGT │
              │            │Perform paired│    └──────────────┘
              │            │ comparison   │            │
              │            └──────────────┘            │
              │                     │                  │
              └─────────────────────┴──────────────────┘
                               │
                               ▼
                      ( Possible causes
                         established and
                        consensus reached )
```

Tool Selection Flowchart for Possible Cause Generation and Consensus Reaching Explained

First, decide which problem needs possible cause generation and define the objective of the session. Typical applications are generating ideas about which problem to solve, possible causes for a problem, and possible solutions to a problem.

Next, assess the situation in which the possible cause generation will occur and select an appropriate approach. Typical considerations are allowing everyone to participate properly, anonymity, complexity, and so forth. If there is a chance that any member might dominate the group, use brainwriting instead of brainstorming. Both brainstorming and brainwriting are characterized as structured approaches with defined rules that support the main objective of generating as many ideas as possible.

After the generation is completed, decide whether a prioritization of the generated ideas is necessary. If not, the possible cause generation and consensus stage is finished. If so, assess whether it is appropriate to analyze the entire set of ideas all at once. The purpose of this assessment is to select between the nominal group technique or paired comparisons. The main purpose of the nominal group technique is to facilitate a form of brainstorming in which all participants have the same vote when selecting solutions, while the idea behind paired comparison is that single decisions are easier to make than selecting among a large number.

Problem and Cause Data Collection Tool Selection

Problem and cause data collection is a set of generic tools and techniques that help in the collection of data related to a problem and its probable causes. They help render the data collection systematic, efficient, and effective. A flowchart for the problem and cause data collection stage is shown below, and is explained on the following page.

Problem
solving

Root cause
analysis

Problem
understanding

Possible cause
generation
and consensus
reaching

Problem and
cause
data collection

Possible cause
analysis

Cause-and-
effect
analysis

Tool selection

Case Business
Quality Travel

Tool Selection Flowchart for Problem and Cause Data Collection Explained

Based on the outcome of the possible cause generation and consensus reaching stage, use a problem and its possible causes as the starting point of the problem and cause data collection stage.

Next, assess whether it is necessary to collect data from the entire population. Typical considerations are the amount of data needed, the nature of the population, the costs involved, and so on. If using a smaller population is acceptable, use sampling. The main purpose of sampling is to allow drawing conclusions about a larger group based on a smaller sample, as long as you are aware of the sample's limitations.

Finally, assess whether you will collect data from respondents or through recording events that occur. In the former case, use surveys. In the latter, a check sheet is an appropriate approach. Surveys are used to collect data from different respondent groups while a check sheet is used to ensure that all data is registered correctly.

Possible Cause Analysis Tool Selection

Possible cause analysis is about making the most out of all the data collected about the problem. When analyzing the same set of data from different angles, many different conclusions might emerge. Some of these might uncover the problem's causes, others not; thus it is important to have a number of data analysis tools available. A flowchart for the possible cause analysis stage is shown below and explained on the following page.

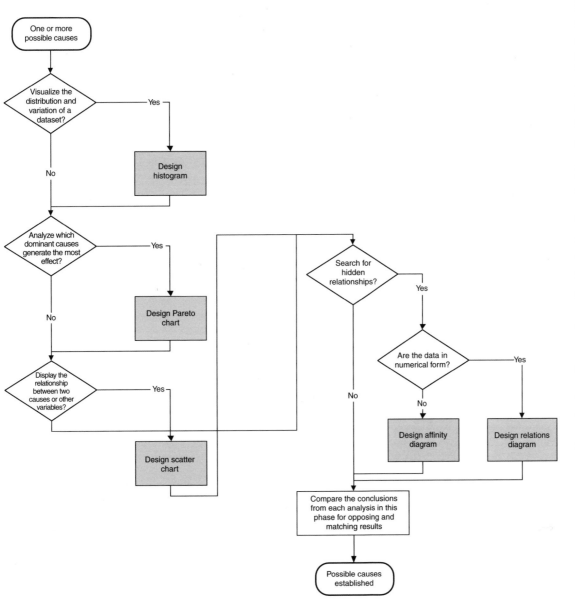

Tool Selection Flowchart for Possible Cause Analysis Explained

Based on the outcome of the problem and cause data collection stage, use one or more data sets pertaining to the problem at hand and its possible causes as the starting point for the possible cause analysis stage.

First, assess whether it is useful to visually display the distribution and variation of a data set. If so, design a histogram.

Second, ask yourself whether it is useful to display the dominant causes that generate the most effects. If so, use a Pareto chart.

Third, determine whether it is useful to display the relationship between two causes or other variables. If so, create a scatter chart.

Fourth, assess whether it is useful to search for relationships among the variables and causes that might be hidden or obscure. If this is not useful, the possible cause analysis stage is finished. If it could be useful, ask whether the data are on a numerical form or not. If they are, design a relations diagram. If not, use an affinity diagram instead.

The conclusions from each analysis at this stage should be compared for opposing or matching results.

The conclusions from the possible cause analysis stage are then brought into the cause-and-effect analysis stage.

Cause-and-Effect Analysis Tool Selection

The cause-and-effect analysis stage is at the heart of the root cause analysis. As previously mentioned, root cause analysis is not one single approach; neither is this group of tools. It contains a few tools that combine to make up an in-depth analysis of the problem's root cause(s). A flowchart for the cause-and-effect analysis stage is shown below, and is explained on the following page.

```
          ┌──────────────────┐
          │ Set of possible  │
          │     causes       │
          └──────────────────┘
                   │
                   ▼
            ╱───────────────╲
           ╱   Additional    ╲        Yes      ┌──────────────────┐
          ⟨ possible causes   ⟩─────────────▶  │  Use cause-and-  │
           ╲     exist?      ╱                  │   effect chart   │
            ╲───────────────╱                   └──────────────────┘
                   │ No                                  │
                   ▼◀───────────────────────────────────┘
            ╱───────────────╲
           ╱  Analyze which  ╲       Yes       ┌──────────────────┐
          ⟨ possible causes   ⟩────────────▶   │   Use matrix     │
           ╲ impact the      ╱                 │    diagram       │
            ╲ problem most?  ╱                  └──────────────────┘
                   │ No                                  │
                   ▼◀───────────────────────────────────┘
            ╱───────────────╲
           ╱  Do higher level ╲      Yes       ┌──────────────────┐
          ⟨ causes exist?      ⟩───────────▶   │   Use five whys  │
           ╲                  ╱                 └──────────────────┘
            ╲───────────────╱                          │
                   │ No                                │
                   ▼◀──────────────────────────────────┘
          ┌──────────────────┐
          │   Root cause     │
          │     found        │
          └──────────────────┘
```

Problem solving

Root cause analysis

Problem understanding

Possible cause generation and consensus reaching

Problem and cause data collection

Possible cause analysis

Cause-and-effect analysis

Tool selection

Case Business Quality Travel

Problem
solving

Root cause
analysis

Problem
understanding

Possible cause
generation
and consensus
reaching

Problem and
cause
data collection

Possible cause
analysis

Cause-and-
effect
analysis

Tool selection

Case Business
Quality Travel

Tool Selection Flowchart for Cause-and-Effect Analysis Explained

Based on the outcome of the possible cause analysis stage, a set of possible causes constitutes the starting point for the cause-and-effect analysis stage.

First ask, "Is it likely that there are additional possible causes to be found?" If the answer is yes—even a hesitant yes—run a cause-and-effect chart session.

Second ask, "Is it useful to analyze which of the possible causes seem to impact the problem the most?" If yes, use a matrix diagram.

Third ask, "Is it likely that there are higher level causes to the problem, beyond those already identified?" Again, even a hesitant confirmation should lead to the application of the five whys tool.

Finally, check to determine if the conclusions from the cause-and-effect analysis stage are true and relevant conclusions about the root cause of the problem being analyzed.

Tool Summary

The following table summarizes some key aspects of the tools that have been presented in this book. When deciding which tool to use, use this table for guidance, but remember that the specific situation in which the tool will be used also impacts its suitability.

Stage/Tool	Purpose	Strengths/Advantages	Weaknesses/Difficulties
Problem understanding			
Flowchart	Understand the flow of activities in a process	• Easy to use • Uses graphics	• Difficult to decide on the level of detail
Critical incident	Understand what are the most troublesome symptoms	• Allows everyone to participate • Generates many ideas	• Requires trust and openness
Spider chart	Compare performance with external references	• Easily understandable graphic presentation	• Difficult to obtain the necessary data
Performance matrix	Prioritize problems or symptoms to attack	• Leads to a structured analysis • Graphic approach	• Requires subjective assessments
Possible cause generation and consensus reaching			
Brainstorming	Generate as many ideas as possible	• Easy to use • Involves many people	• One or a few people can dominate • No anonymity is possible
Brainwriting	Generate as many ideas as possible	• Involves many people • Enables anonymity	• Can be less spontaneous than brainstorming
Nominal group technique	Prioritize ideas	• Easy to use • Allows everyone equal vote	• Can be difficult to choose among many alternatives
Paired comparisons	Prioritize ideas	• Requires comparing only two alternatives	• With many alternatives, the exercise becomes infeasible due to a high number of pairs
Problem and cause data collection			
Sampling	Gain a representative sample from a large population	• Minimizes the data collection effort	• Difficult to decide on the type of sampling and sample size • The sample may not be representative

Continued on next page

Problem solving

Root cause analysis

Problem understanding

Possible cause generation and consensus reaching

Problem and cause data collection

Possible cause analysis

Cause-and-effect analysis

Tool selection

Case Business Quality Travel

Problem
solving

Root cause
analysis

Problem
understanding

Possible cause
generation
and consensus
reaching

Problem and
cause
data collection

Possible cause
analysis

Cause-and-
effect
analysis

➤ Tool selection

Case Business
Quality Travel

Stage/Tool	Purpose	Strengths/Advantages	Weaknesses/Difficulties
Surveys	Collect data from respondents	• Allows collection of large amounts of data	• Good surveys are difficult to design • Often low response rate
Check sheet	Register data in a systematic fashion	• Easy to use • Ensures all data are captured	• Data categories not specified may be overlooked
Possible cause analysis			
Histogram	Portray data graphically	• Easy to see patterns • Uses graphics	• Difficult to identify classes
Pareto chart	Find the few elements causing most effects	• Striking graphics	• Multiple axes in the same chart
Scatter chart	Find relationships between two variables	• Easy to comprehend graphics	• Difficult to select the independent and dependent variable
Relations diagram	Find relationships among many elements	• Provides a structured approach • Gives a clear graphic picture	• Relies on subjective assessments • The diagram could become quite complex
Affinity diagram	Find relationships otherwise not easily seen	• Can reveal hard to recognize relationships	• Requires creativity, patience, and previous experience • Less structured
Cause-and-effect analysis			
Cause-and-effect chart	Generate and group problem causes	• Easy to use • Promotes structure *and* creativity	• One or a few people many dominate the exercise
Matrix diagram	Analyze causal relationships	• Provides structure to the analysis • Displays combined impact of factors	• Relies on subjective assessments • Some diagram types can be complex to use
Five whys	Identify chains of cause-and-effect	• Easy to use • Finds the root cause	• Requires some creativity and deep knowledge of the problem

Case Business Quality Travel

In the previous chapters, we have presented a number of tools for root cause analysis, guidelines for selecting them, and some examples of their use. In this chapter, we present an example of the integrated use of these tools at the travel agent Business Quality Travel.

Business Quality Travel

Business Quality Travel (BQT) is a medium-sized travel agency located in Grand Peak. BQT has 25 employees and a turnover of $30 million a year. The majority of BQT's employees are women between 25 and 40 years old. BQT has a rather flat organization with three levels: manager, head of groups, and operators. BQT's core business is business travel but it also offers guidance for leisure trips. Although BQT is located in downtown Grand Peak, most customers prefer to order their trips by telephone. The number of trips ordered by e-mail and on the Internet has risen recently, but the numbers are still low. Trips can also be ordered by fax, but still approximately 90 percent of the trips are booked by phone. Often, the traveler calls to order, but secretaries order about 20 percent of the trips.

FRAME AGREEMENTS AND PROBLEMS

BQT is trying to establish closer relationships with its key customers and has recently established frame agreements with nine large companies. The agreements state that BQT is the preferred and only travel agent for these companies. In return, BQT provides extensive discounts on the tickets these companies buy. In addition, these companies have access to a dedicated hotline for ordering tickets. A group of BQT's employees work only with these key companies, of which one is a very large customer.

Lately, BQT has been experiencing some difficulties. The absenteeism due to sickness among the employees has risen. The internal conflict level at BQT has also increased. Every other day, the manager spots indications of a poor working environment. The annual spring dinner for all employees had to be cancelled due to a low sign-up rate. The main problem, however, was that the manager has received some complaints from customers regarding the service level at BQT. Often, it was impossible to get through on the phone to an operator, and the service provided (when they finally got hold of one) was not adequate. Some customers had even experienced rude comments from BQT's employees.

Problem Understanding at BQT

The general manager arranged a meeting with the selected employee representative, and they agreed that the company was facing a serious problem. They agreed to form a group to analyze the situation and find the root cause. The group consisted of the general manager, Elizabeth; the employee representative, John; a senior travel agent operator, Ann; and a junior operator, Deb. Among the group's first decisions: (a) to use the methodologies presented in this book to solve the problem; (b) the problem might be related to the working environment in one way or another; and (c) the group would meet frequently and keep an open mind during the process. Ann was selected as chairperson of the group and John was selected as the group's secretary.

Problem
solving

Root cause
analysis

Problem
understanding

Possible cause
generation
and consensus
reaching

Problem and
cause
data collection

Possible cause
analysis

Cause-and-
effect
analysis

Tool selection

Case Business
Quality Travel

FLOWCHART AND CRITICAL INCIDENT

As the current process was not properly documented, the first thing the group had to do was to draw a flowchart to document the current process. The flowchart is shown on the following page.

The next question for the group was whether they really knew what was causing the most trouble. No one in the group could give a definite answer to this question, and thus they performed a critical incident analysis. The results were

- Did not know how to handle requests

- No time for breaks

- Could not find the data in the computer-based system

- Handling only complex travels

- Headaches

- Did not have time to get back to customers

- Work too much overtime

- Insufficient information from customers

BQT Flowchart

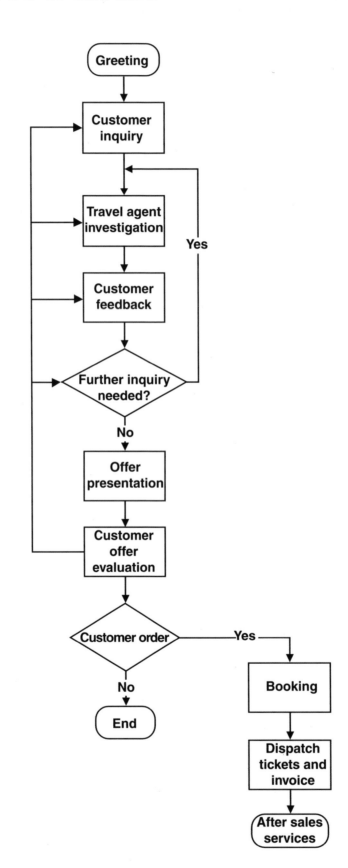

Problem
solving

Root cause
analysis

Problem
understanding

Possible cause
generation
and consensus
reaching

Problem and
cause
data collection

Possible cause
analysis

Cause-and-
effect
analysis

Tool selection

Case Business
Quality Travel

BQT Performance Matrix

The next question the group discussed was whether any type of external comparison could be useful. The manager suggested that other travel agents might have similar problems, and the group agreed that this might be a good idea. The manager talked with managers of other travel agencies he knew, and it seemed that about half of them were experiencing similar difficulties, but none of the managers knew exactly why. The type of difficulties varied somewhat from agency to agency, and some were considering analysis of the situation.

In the end, the team completed the problem understanding stage by designing a performance matrix, as shown below. Based on the matrix, they concluded that the main problem seemed to be the poor overall availability of BQT's operators to its customers.

Problem solving

Root cause analysis

Problem understanding

Possible cause generation and consensus reaching

Problem and cause data collection

Possible cause analysis

Cause-and-effect analysis

Tool selection

Case Business Quality Travel

Possible Cause Generation and Consensus Reaching at BQT

At the next meeting of the root cause analysis group, the team looked at the possible cause generation and consensus stage.

To decide whether to use brainstorming or brainwriting, each member received a piece of paper on which they wrote S or W. It was agreed that if any-one wrote W, brainwriting would be applied.

The results were three S's and one W, and the results from the brainwriting are shown below.

RESULTS FROM THE BRAINWRITING

The assumed main problem was determined as

- Operator availability to customers.

  Proposed possible causes included:

- Low capacity
- Frequent leaves of absence
- Customers not knowing what they want—the booking taking a long time
- Not enough knowledge to handle requests
- New technology
- Interface with the booking system is slow
- No incentives to work harder
- Increased percentage of customers wanting complex travel routes

Problem and Cause Data Collection at BQT

Problem solving

Root cause analysis

Problem understanding

Possible cause generation and consensus reaching

Problem and cause data collection

Possible cause analysis

Cause-and-effect analysis

Tool selection

Case Business Quality Travel

After an initial assessment, the group concluded that the amount of data available concerning the problem and its causes was very limited. Ann argued that they should use some kind of check sheet to collect data from the processes. Elizabeth agreed, while John and Deb felt it would be appropriate to send a survey to the employees. After a heated discussion, Deb suggested they use both; the others agreed. The check sheet was designed to collect data on the time the travel agent operators spent on each task in the booking process. The survey was designed to collect the views the travel agent operators had on the suggested possible causes. The data was collected over a one-week period.

QUESTIONS ASKED IN THE SURVEY

Dear employee,

Our company has been experiencing some problems lately, and a group has been established to find the root cause of these problems. So far we have established that the major problem is the availability of BQT's employees to its customers. Based on this assumption, we are conducting this small survey. Please answer each question by checking the appropriate box.

- On a scale from 1 (poor) to 5 (good), how do you assess our availability?
- Which of the following items contributes most to the lack of availability?

☐ 1. Low capacity

☐ 2. Frequent leaves of absence

☐ 3. Customers not knowing what they want—booking taking a long time

☐ 4. Not enough knowledge to handle requests

☐ 5. New technology

☐ 6. Interface with the booking system is slow

☐ 7. No incentives to work hard

☐ 8. Percentage of customers wanting complex travel routes increasing

Problem
solving

Root cause
analysis

Problem
understanding

Possible cause
generation
and consensus
reaching

Problem and
cause
data collection

Possible cause
analysis

Cause-and-
effect
analysis

Tool selection

Case Business
Quality Travel

Possible Cause Analysis at BQT

The check sheet data on time consumption in the booking process revealed very few interesting findings. For the survey data on the employees' beliefs in terms of what caused the poor availability, a simple histogram-like chart was produced to visualize the response distribution, as shown below.

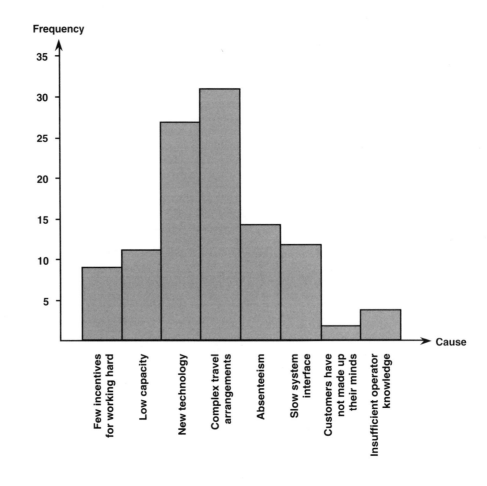

From the chart, two obvious candidates stood out in terms of being important problem causes, namely

- New technology and the problems related to the use of it.

- A movement toward more complex travel arrangements, as the customers were now booking simple trips themselves via the Internet.

Cause-and-Effect Analysis at BQT

After having been excited about finding the apparent solutions to the problems' causes, the team decided that perhaps their work was not yet over. When pondering these two causes, they found that there probably were additional higher level causes, and decided to employ the five whys approach as a final step in the investigation. The result, after four whys, is shown below:

Low operator availability

Why?   **New technology and complex travel arrangements**

  Why?   **Pressure for efficiency and customers booking simpler trips directly from the airlines**

    Why?   **Low margins on tickets and the airlines often offer better discounts**

      Why?   **The ticket commission from the airlines has been reduced significantly the last two years**

THE ROOT CAUSE

Even if the analysis could be brought no further than four whys, the team felt absolutely certain that they had really uncovered the true root cause of the problem. When they suddenly realized that many of the problems were in fact caused, directly or indirectly, by the dramatic cuts in the ticket commissions from the airlines, the pieces finally fell into place.

These cuts had produced immense pressure to make up for the lost income. This had produced a very stressful climate, both at BQT and many other travel agencies, which in turn has led to the introduction of new technologies. As customers started to approach the travel agents only when they had questions about more complex trips, each inquiry took longer. All in all, this caused the operators to spend more time on the phone with clients, while earning less per call. This materialized into a problem visible to the customers, that is, that it was difficult to get through to an operator.

How to solve this problem is a completely different story and one we will not present here. However, having found the root cause, BQT was well on its way to solving its problem!

Further Reading and Additional Resources

This section contains an overview of the literature that deals with root cause analysis as a whole or sub-topics of root cause analysis. Some deals with the topic differently than we have, or deals with it in more detail. You will also find a guide to additional software resources that might be useful during the analysis.

Further Reading

This list includes some suggested reading materials that treat the tools presented in this book (as well as others) in more detail.

Ammerman, Max. 1998. *The Root Cause Analysis Handbook: A Simplified Approach to Identifying, Correcting, and Reporting Workplace Errors.* Quality Resources.

Eastman Kodak Company. 1990. *Quality Leadership Process Guidebook.* Rochester, NY: Eastman Kodak Company.

Gitlow, Howard, Alan Oppenheim, and Rosa Oppenheim. 1995. *Quality Management: Tools and Methods for Improvement.* Burr Ridge, IL: Irwin.

Lawlor, Alan. 1985. *Productivity Improvement Manual.* Aldershot, England: Gower Publishing.

Mizuno, Shigeru, ed. 1988. *Management for Quality Improvement: The 7 New QC Tools.* Cambridge, MA: Productivity Press.

Scholtes, Peter R. 1988. *The Team Handbook: How to Use Teams to Improve Quality.* Madison, WI: Joiner.

Straker, David. 1995. *A Toolbook for Quality Improvement and Problem Solving.* London, England: Prentice-Hall.

Swanson, Roger C. 1995. *The Quality Improvement Handbook: Team Guide to Tools and Techniques.* London, England: Kogan Page.

Wilson, Paul F., Larry D. Dell, and Gaylord F. Anderson. 1993. *Root Cause Analysis: A Tool for Total Quality Management.* Milwaukee, WI: American Society for Quality Control.

Wilson, Paul F. 1992. *Root Cause Analysis Workbook.* Milwaukee, WI: American Society for Quality Control.

Additional Resources

Software tools that could be useful at different stages in root cause analysis are listed below. Since this book is not an advertising channel for different suppliers' software, no descriptions have been given. Essential information such as web addresses, company addresses, and so on, is provided, but for some of the products, the list is not complete. In addition, it should be noted that the information in the list will not be accurate indefinitely.

- Visio Professional, http://www.visio.com/index.html
  Visio Corporation, 2211 Elliott Avenue, Seattle, WA 98121-1691, USA
  Telephone: 206-956-6000
  Fax: 206-956-6001

- Micrografx's FlowCharter, http://www.micrografx.com/frames.asp?s=2
  Micrografx, Inc., 1303 East Arapaho, Richardson, TX 75081, USA
  Telephone: 972-234-1769
  Fax: 716-873-0906
  E-mail: hr@micrografx.com

- The Memory Jogger Software, http://www.goalqpc.com/WELCOME.html
  GOAL/QPC, 2 Manor Parkway, Salem, NH 03079, USA
  Telephone: 800-207-5813 (in the US & Canada)
  or 603-893-1944 (worldwide)
  Fax: 603-870-9122
  E-mail: servicex@goalqpc.com

- StatGraphics Plus, http://www.statgraphics.com/
  Manugistics, Inc., 2115 East Jefferson Street, Rockville, MD 20852, USA
  Telephone: 800-592-0050, ext. 900
  E-mail: sgsales@manu.com

- SAS/QC software, http://www.sas.com/SASHome.html
  SAS Institute Inc., SAS Campus Drive, Cary, NC 27513-2414, USA
  Telephone: 919-677-8000
  Fax: 919-677-4444

- allClear, http://www.allclear2000.com/
  SIMCOM Software Company, P.O. Box 801, Springwood, Queensland, Australia 4127
  Telephone: 61 7 3841 3999
  Fax: 61 7 3341 7579

- AutoCad, http://www.autodesk.com/
  Autodesk, Inc., 20400 Stevens Creek Boulevard, Cupertino, CA
      95014-2217, USA
  Telephone: 408-517-1700
  Fax: 408-517-1757

- CADKEY, http://www.cadkey.com/
  Baystate Technologies, 33 Boston Post Road West, Marlborough, MA
      01752, USA
  Telephone: 508-229-2020
  Fax: 508-229-2121

- PFT for Windows, http://www.iqd.com/index.htm
  Integrated Quality Dynamics, Inc., 3848 Carson Street,
      Suite #216, Torrance, CA 90503, USA
  Telephone: 310-540-6142
  Fax: 310-540-6392
  E-mail: iqd@iqd.com

- ParaMind, http://www.paramind.net/
  ParaMind Software, P.O. Box 27401, Seattle, WA 98125-2401, USA
  E-mail: paramind@paramind.net

Index

The index contains an alphabetical list of keywords with a reference to the page numbers where the keywords are explained in more detail. Use the index to quickly find the topics you are looking for.